The Spartan Mindset

Praise for *The Spartan Mindset*

When I researched the secrets weeds use to grow, spread, conquer, and defend their turf, I saw the full power of mindset required to succeed in any field of competition. What I appreciate about *The Spartan Mindset* by Coach Reed Maltbie is his deep dive into the Spartan language of mindset to deepen our resolve to win. I appreciate Coach Reed's perspective as well, basing it on the Spartans, who were, after all, total weeds. Without a fierce Spartan mindset, success never comes. With it, success is all but guaranteed.

-**Stu Heinecke,** bestselling author of *How to Grow Your Business Like a Weed* and *How to Get a Meeting with Anyone*

Reed takes us on a journey of self-reflection as we are challenged to consider our use of language and the impact it can have, both positive and negative. Using real world examples and scenarios he does a brilliant job of setting the scene, painting the picture and then getting us to reflect on our own day to day environments. Effective communication is a key strand in the work we do with organizations, coaches and parents and this book will certainly help all stakeholders in how we all use our language to build positive relationships and ensure the best outcomes for those that we encounter.

-**Gordon MacLelland,** CEO, WWPIS
(Working with Parents in Sport)

Reed delivers a succinct, attention-grabbing, highly relevant influence manual for coaches, parents and leaders of any level. *The Spartan Mindset* is practical, profound and immediately applicable for those of us who seek to encourage and empower others.

-**Justin Bredeman,** CEO & partner,
Soccer Shots Franchising, LLC

One word in *The Spartan Mindset* caused me to leap out of my chair and sprint around the block like a raging bull to burn off some energy . . . and that was just in Chapter 1. Wait until you get to [Chapter] 7. Words can be abstract or they can be concrete. The words and principles in Reed's book hit like a pallet of cinder blocks dropped from a crane. If you lead a family, team, or business, you would do well to devour this book and implement its wisdom in your thoughts and speech.

-**Andrew Miner,** entrepreneur

The Spartan Mindset is a powerful and fun read. As an experienced coach, there were a number of topics in this book that I was already familiar with, but what's incredibly powerful about Coach Reed's writing is that it provides the reader an opportunity to look at a familiar topic in a completely new way. Coach Reed does a masterful job of not only explaining a concept, but also providing relatable anecdotes that show how easily applicable a topic is to any performance situation at any level. The style and tone of the book is incredibly similar to Patrick Lencioni, and like Lencioni, I came away saying, "I didn't think of that in *that* way." I guarantee that even experienced coaches and leaders will read this book and find impactful adjustments in their craft.

-**Stu Gilfillen,** director of Education, US Sailing

The Spartan Mindset is a must read for any coach/teacher/parent out there that want to make a difference in a child's life! What we say and how we say it effects our brains in more ways than we realize, and if we are not careful we can build or destroy people around us. If you know Coach Reed, you'll hear him in every word of this book. The passion and love he has for words and teaching comes through every line and page. If you want to grow as a parent, coach, teacher, you will apply every word to your day to day. I did, and it changed my life.

-**Joel Franco,** founder of Chesapeake Films and director, *Where Our Children Play*

If. Don't. Try. These are mundane words at first glance. But Coach Reed Maltbie, in *The Spartan Mindset*, schools coaches and leaders (in the best of ways) on how to pause, choose words wisely, and transform their teams for the better. Through straightforward yet relatable stories and advice, Coach Reed outfits readers with a new way of speaking—and coaching. If you work with people, it's time to learn "The Spartan Mindset."

-**Cortney Donelson,** owner and principal writer, vocem LLC; author of *The Outlier's Choice: Why Living an Uncomfortable Life is Worth It,* and retired tennis instructor

THE
SPARTAN
MINDSET

MASTERING THE
LANGUAGE OF
EXCELLENCE

REED MALTBIE

NEW YORK

LONDON • NASHVILLE • MELBOURNE • VANCOUVER

THE *SPARTAN* MINDSET

Mastering the Language of Excellence

Published in New York, New York, by Morgan James Publishing. Morgan James is a trademark of Morgan James, LLC. www.MorganJamesPublishing.com

Proudly distributed by Ingram Publisher Services.

Morgan James BOGO™

A **FREE** ebook edition is available for you or a friend with the purchase of this print book.

CLEARLY SIGN YOUR NAME ABOVE

Instructions to claim your free ebook edition:
1. Visit MorganJamesBOGO.com
2. Sign your name CLEARLY in the space above
3. Complete the form and submit a photo of this entire page
4. You or your friend can download the ebook to your preferred device

ISBN 9781631959981 paperback
ISBN 9781631959998 ebook
Library of Congress Control Number: 2022941343

Cover Design by:
Rachel Lopez
www.r2cdesign.com

Interior Design by:
Chris Treccani
www.3dogcreative.net

Morgan James is a proud partner of Habitat for Humanity Peninsula and Greater Williamsburg. Partners in building since 2006.

Get involved today! Visit MorganJamesPublishing.com/giving-back

To my wife, Amy,
Your love, encouragement, and support made this book possible.
Without your willingness to "take a boat to the end of the world,"
it would have remained unwritten. I hope the words in this book
transform other lives like you have mine.

To my children, Julia, Cooper, and Cameron,
May the words in your life grow a garden filled with empowerment, joy, courage, and love. And if some words don't belong in
this garden, may you have the awareness and strength to not water
those words.

Table of Contents

Acknowledgments

One of the constants that I learned throughout my sporting and coaching journey is that no one ever reaches the summit on their own. It takes a team of people, many working hard in the background, for that moment of ascension. Along the way, I have played the lead roles and the support roles, and both are wholly fulfilling on their own.

I also know how important it is to recognize those who have supported your journey. This book was only made possible through the mentorship, advice, support, and dedicated work of so many amazing people in my life. Without them, the book would have never made it to print.

First, to my editorial and publishing team, I want to thank you for the dedication and encouragement. You all showed so much patience and grace as I learned the nuances of what it takes to publish a manuscript. Thank you to David Hancock and Morgan James Publishing for believing in me and to Jim Howard, Chris Howard, Emily Madison, Amber Parrott, Jessica Burton-Moran, Lauren Howard, Jodi Henderson, and Naomi Chellis—my author support team for your tireless work to get this ready for print.

To Michael Ebeling, my agent, for your suggestions, edits, support, and bringing me to the Morgan James family. You were the only agent, of the hundreds I queried, who responded to me. It took us about 8 years before I had the right book and here we are.

Thank you, Cortney Donelson, my amazing editor. You shaped my rough manuscript into an amazing book that flows, has character, and captures the essence of my passion for words. You did so much more than editing, too—advised me on format, helped with quotes, and walked me through every single step. The best compliment I can give you is that one of my friends said they could hear me speaking in every paragraph; you helped me put my passion into print!

This book's journey didn't start in 2017 when I took on the challenge to write a book in a month. This is the culmination of a lifetime of mentorship, guidance, encouragement, and support from so many people whose words have echoed positively in my life.

To those mentors who cultivated and stoked the passion for learning and language. Mrs. Westrich, who reviewed and edited my first screenplay and helped me bring it to life in the most campy and cheesiest of student-produced movies . . . if twelve-year-old me can create a movie, forty-eight-year-old me can publish a book.

Mr. Hussong, Mr. Coral, and Mr. Downie, who developed my love of language and reading. They ignited that fire, and it still burns brightly today. I also tell Mr. Downie's stories of his travels every chance I get.

To Dr. Epes and Dr. Manning, who further expanded my love of language through their inspiring and insightful Humanities lectures at Davidson College. One particular moment that stands out was listening for sixty minutes to a riveting and detailed lecture from the Medieval era from Dr. Epes and then looking at his notes to realize they were blank. He did it all from memory! To Cole Barton and John Kello, who gave me the strong psychology background that led to my curiosity in how the brain effects physical performance.

To Dr. Vealey for being an amazing mentor in graduate school and Dr. Ingham (I miss you dearly), for reminding me I can be "too verbose." Both of you taught me the nuances of research and distilling important information into bite-sized, practical snippets. And to Susie Grybowski, for being my amazing mentor teacher who taught me as much about life as she did about managing a classroom. Those elementary students have no idea how lucky they are!

The person and coach I am today is a direct reflection of those who coached me throughout my career. Coaches like Donny Smith and my father, Bill Maltbie, who recognized early in my playing career that the dialogue in my head needed to be guided to help me succeed. My father was my first coach, and it was my greatest honor to be coached by him. I grew up watching him coach every sport under the sun and hung on his every word. It was only fitting he started me on this sporting path. To answer his question about whether I regret choosing the sport that was my weakest one, I don't regret a thing – my purpose wasn't for being a lifelong athlete, it was for spending my life coaching coaches. Better Coaching for a Better World.

Coach Houchen and Coach West, who filled my junior high years with the language of excellence and taught me how to lead others.

Coach Paul Rockwood, who got me into coaching and told me it would change my life. He could not have been more right! His words continue to echo every day, and my greatest joy was getting to see him coach my children.

Coach Bobby Kramig, who had poured words of encouragement into me since I was eight years old and was willing to take me under his wing as a graduate assistant at Miami University.

The other coaches who acted as friends, colleagues, confidants, and mentors: Andy Szucs, Jon Caldwell, Bill Stoeckel, Rajiv Soman, Dave McIver, Andy Boyd, Mark Hecquet, Shelly Krisfalusi, Russel Lewis, Yonas Asmeron, Jack Perkins, Tom Eckart, Ron Brickley, Bryan Daniel, Alexa Bencic (my camp co-leader) and so many others. I cherished every moment I got to coach alongside you. To my STAR family, especially Dave Crowe and Amy Hagedorn, for letting me be part of their amazing journey (#WeAreStar).

To the teams and soccer clubs I worked with over the years that helped me learn the true power of the language of excellence: Fairfield Optimist Soccer Club, Davidson College Women's Club Soccer, Miami University Soccer, Gainesville Soccer Association, Harrison Soccer Club, Hammer FC (I got to coach one of these players as a youth and then over a decade later as a Professional player!) all my Lakota-Monroe teams and families (including the famous GOLD "warrior mindset" team that has served as the example in many workshops), St. Xavier High School Soccer, the entire Soccer Shots organization (especially Liz Barker-Aquino, Jamie Tunnell and the East San Diego team – that move was a real catalyst), STAR SC (we proved you can put the kids first, focus more on creating better people beyond the game, have fun, and still win games), Cincinnati Saints (I can actually say I have won a game as a Professional coach), and Talawanda Soccer (who gave me the greatest upset win of my career).

To those who have been partners of mine in the journey to create a better sporting experience for our children: Kevin Greene and all of US Lacrosse—Karl Norton, Gordon MacLelland, Joel Franco, John Kessel—and USA Volleyball, Stu Gilfillen, Katie Ouilette, and John Pearce at US Sailing, Blair Overman, Janel Zarkowsky, Meredith Dart, and Chris Childers at the Siebel Sailors Program (we built an amazing youth sailing experience together and you taught me the Zen of sailing), Louis-Pierre Maineville and Ontario Volleyball, Mark Hesse and USA Swimming, Glen Cundari and PGA Canada, Kevin Kirk and the PGA, Dave Kelly and Ontario Soccer, Joe Bonnett and USA Hockey, Nadine Dubina and the US Olympic and Paralympic Committee, Luther Rauk, JP Nerbun, Mark O'Sullivan, Matt Young of QSH, Cesar Coronel, Maureen Monte, Ken Willner, Dave Marlow, Sam Snow and US Youth Soccer, Adrian Parish and Kentucky Youth Soccer, Casey Mann and Nebraska Soccer, Warren Abrahams, Dave and Adam Wright from Player Development Project, Coach Craig Gunn, Dan Cottrell, Stu

Armstrong, Jen Fraser, V.J. Stanley, Dr. Rob Bell, Tyler Hardrick (I love watching you teach golf), Dan Abrahams, Phil Schoen, and so many others who have worked tirelessly alongside me to create true change in youth sports.

To Dr. Jane Nelsen, we were put together by sheer coincidence and the fact you decided I was "that coach" who should co-author *Positive Discipline Tools for Coaches* meant the world to me. Your advice and encouragement bolstered me in a time when I needed it most, and though I may have been instinctually using PD Tools all my life, like a great Jedi teacher, you helped me hone the craft. I will always be grateful to you for your mentorship.

To Stu Heinecke, Oren Klaff, Justin Bredeman, and Andrew Miner who were also willing to review along with Stu Gilfillen, Gordon MacLelland, and Joel Franco. There was definitely some anxiety to put my soul on paper for the world to see, but your testimonials gave me strength and courage.

To Daniel Coyle, who somehow found me and sent me an advance copy of his groundbreaking book The Talent Code. I still recall opening the package and thinking "what author would want me to review their book?" It was life changing. It laid the groundwork for me to under-stand how the brain develops pathways of skill and how words can affect the pathways. Thank you!

To Carmine Gallo, without your book, *Talk Like TED*, I would never have had such a great TEDx experience and would never have crossed paths with you. That TEDx Talk was the catalyst for so much positive change in my life and for me continuing to advocate on the behalf of athletes all over the world. Thank you!

Finally, to those who always provide the most support and who expect nothing in return, my friends and family. My wife, Amy, my children—Julia, Cooper, and Cameron—and my daughter's spouse, Lily, who hopes this book becomes standard classroom reading. A few of my amazing friends, who have been sounding boards, golf buddies, camping and hiking partners, and confidants over the years as this book came to life—Dave Donnelly, Dennis Buck, Jackie and Chris Pankau, Chad Denham, Joel Franco. You have always been my sounding board, my counselors, and my testing grounds when I was coming up with some other crazy project or idea.

To my parents, Bill and Linda, who have loved and supported me every step of the way (who else's parents come to the youth soccer games they coach?). They didn't have a child playing in the game, yet there they were, cheering me, the coach, on from the other sideline. To my brother, Bill, for his support over the years, driving in the snow to see me speak two hours from home. To Grandpa Barth, the man with whom I share a very striking resemblance and demeanor. I was your little doppelganger, and I learned so much about being a good human from you in such a short time. I hope Reedo Torpedo did you proud as a man.

There are so many more people who were part of this journey, and I hope you continue to be part of it. As I was once told by my Humanities professors: "If I have seen further it is by standing on the shoulders of giants." (Isaac Newton) Let's hope someone stands on our shoulders to see even further tomorrow.

SECTION 1

The Survivor's Imperative

Chapter 1

A Message to Sparta

If we are to understand how words can shape our outcomes and how the use of words can change history, the Spartans are certainly the ultimate word warriors.

The story goes that Philip II of Macedon was driving his forces through Greece, conquering its city-states. He had subdued many of them and was closing in on control of the entire empire.

Emboldened by his recent successes, he turned his attention to the war state of Sparta. History tells us that Sparta is not a group of warriors to be trifled with, no matter how large your army is. If we learned anything from the historical action film, *300*, we know these guys were tough cookies.

However, if there was a time to take a shot at Sparta, it would have been during Philip II's conquest. Sparta, at the time, was in rough shape. Having endured the Battle of Thermopylae, the warriors were depleted, morale was low, they were left without walls, and their city-state was on the verge of becoming more of an afterthought. They were waning, and now was certainly the time for Philip II to take a swing at the weakened group.

He may have sensed this weakened condition, or he did it out of respect for the once-great warriors they were, but Philip II sent a note to Sparta before his attack. His note was simple yet threatening. It read like a perfectly scripted line in a great war movie: "You are advised to submit without further delay, for if I bring my army into your land, I will destroy your farms, slay your people, and raze your city."

This is the kind of threat that gives most men pause. Even the more vicious warriors can consider the damage to the greater number with such a powerful threat, and considering Sparta had been terribly weakened by recent wars and had no walls to protect them, this would be something they would not take lightly.

The Spartans are known for two things. They were one of the fiercest warrior societies ever, and they were men of few words. When they spoke, their words were terse, heavy with meaning, and witty. The brilliant responses of the Spartans in history gave rise to the saying "Laconic phrase" and made *300* one of the easiest movies to quote.

Admit it. You've run around, playing your weekend warrior games, working out in the gym, or playing poker with your friends, saying things like, "Then come and take it" or "Then we shall fight in the shade."[1] When King Leonidas spoke in the movie *300*, web memes tumbled out in droves.

The Spartans considered this a generous offer from Philip. Surrender and spare the people, the crops, the city. Seemed like a fair trade. Definitely an offer you and I would consider . . . but this was Sparta (you know you said that in Girard Butler's voice).

Their response did not disappoint historians the world over. They sent back a one-word reply. *One word.* The fate of a city-state and all of its people hung on that one word. What could they possibly have conveyed with only one word?

Much—because the Spartans knew something Philip had not considered. Words hold great power. They can build up or tear down people. They can start wars, grow relationships, change the meaning of life, implant dreams, and dash all hope. Words, when used properly, can spark amazing success. Words, when used to harm others, will leave an indelible mark of self-doubt and negativity on someone's psyche, often for life.

Words started a revolution here in America. Words separate us from animals. With words, we can bring to life realities that did not exist before. With words, we have the opportunity to motivate the next generation to go beyond our expectations. With words, we can rally a nation to a great cause. If words did not have power, we would not rely on them so much in our everyday lives.

To teach us, to share news, to greet each other, to display love to those we care about, and to end the day on a positive note. Words are one of two things: power or peril. So what could have possibly been conveyed by the Spartans in one single word? How could the fate of generations of a people be held in the balance by just one word? The answer is easy. If you say it, you better mean it, and Philip II knew they meant it.

The Spartans responded to Philip by circling a single word in his note to them: *If.*

If he comes into their state, he will destroy their crops, kill their people, and raze the city. *If.* Not when. One word in Philip's note conveyed his confidence and delivered possibility to his enemies. One word in Philip's sentence gave the Spartans a chance to rally. An opportunity to once again show how "laconic" they could be and inject their men of war, their men of great moral strength, into battle. One word undid Philip's entire campaign.

Philip read the note and took a hard pass. He had given the Spartans a chance to surrender, and instead, they repelled his attack before it could start. Philip showed his hand by not attacking. He must have already held great concern over taking on these living gods, and that single word not only betrayed his deepest fears, but it also emboldened those mighty men of war. He did not have the confidence in his vocabulary to use words like "when" or "after."

Those latter words convey a stronger belief in his own abilities. They direct a future that is already set. As if an afterthought, Philip could have said, "Oh yeah, and when I come in, I will raze your once-great city." Instead of a wholly possible and already visualized future, Philip used *if* to give rise to a doubtful and possibly impossible future. His words caused his peril (or at least the peril of that campaign).

Either the Spartans, in all of their wisdom and insight—known specifically for their insight into the hearts of men—read the note and saw his fear or they had such a bada$$ warrior mindset that they saw the note and no care was given.

I imagine it was a combination of both. You see, even though the Spartans were the warrior-state, the women of Sparta were diplomatic, intelligent, and great learners of human nature. They certainly saw through Philip's bravado to the deeper concern in his words. They certainly knew he sent a message out of respect and with a "dip the toe" mentality. If he was bluffing, why not call his bluff?

I also suspect they truly did not care. They were a warrior state. This is what they were born and raised for—the fight. They sent 300 men to fight all of Xerxes's army, after all. They were the people whose mothers told them to come home carrying the shield or on it (meaning you fight until you win or you die). This was the society that trained boys from day one to do one thing well: to fight.

Of course, they would answer with *if*. It is the most perfect response in all of history to this outright evil threat. No rebuttal prior and no rebuttal since has come close to capturing the true nature of a warrior's brain than that single-word answer. We know of later famous leaders who were aware of the story and also responded in such brazen manners, but the Spartans claim fame for this original, fierce response.

There is no better exchange of words about the power and peril of words related to human performance. If we are to understand how words can shape our outcomes and how the use of words can change history, the Spartans are certainly the ultimate word warriors.

> ## When your language isn't certain, your outcome isn't either.

In one word, they thwarted a threat to their very existence. In one word, a great King's army was halted in its tracks. Not only is this the perfect example of the power of words, but it also encompasses the mere dichotomy of our words: they hold both peril and power. How we use them, how we perceive them, and how we are trained to react to them make all the difference.

If we can learn to harness the true power of words, we can have a profoundly positive impact on the performance of those we lead. *If*.

Chapter 2

The Significance of Words

The impact of words is all at once profound and simple.

If. That one word was all it took to change the course of history for an entire civilization. The Spartans knew the power of one word to avoid death, destruction, and despair. They responded to a mortal threat against their entire population with a single word and thwarted what would have been the end of their legacy.

The Power of Just One Word

Citizens. Thomas Jefferson fully understood how changing one word would shape the future of a nascent American people. He changed "subjects" to "citizens" on the Declaration of Independence and the rest, as they say, was history.

Power. Since one word can change history for a nation, imagine what it could do for you. Would you be more intentional with the words you use if you knew they could have that kind of effect? Words hold immense power, and you can harness the power of certain words to spark peak performance.

Peril. Other words have that tendency to unleash performance peril. Saying them sets off a series of thoughts and actions that sabotage peak performance.

Words. Mere words. They can have a profound impact on how individuals and teams perform. As leaders, we have the power to use words that can transform our people.

The Need to Survive

Well before warriors become fierce and honorable competitors, they must learn to survive in the crucible of competition. Choosing to compete every day for excellence, whether it is on a trading floor, a soccer field, or in a classroom, means a willingness to risk failure, embarrassment, or even injury. This takes guts.

For many of us who started young on the journey of everyday excellence, we fell harder and more often than we would like to recount. Each time we fell, though, there was this imperative to get back up and try again. There is a viral video of a skateboarder who tries a trick thirty-four times before he finally gets it right. Every disastrous fall is caught on tape.

What is most striking about the young man is his spirit. He never waivers in his pursuit of mastery. He never cries out in defeat or allows his pride to give him an excuse for quitting. In fact, with each fall, he seems more emboldened, more resilient, and certainly more resolved to master the move.

Near the end of his evolution as a warrior, the viewer can see a breakthrough. He falls and stands up quickly. Looking at the camera, he shows undeterred confidence and declares that he has figured it out, finally. The fall led to a revelation about how to get it right. His energy for that last attempt was as high, if not surpassing the energy of the very first time he tried it.

In those moments, he was surviving. Falling in pain, ego battered, his choice was to flee or to fight. Certainly, his amygdala was going to great lengths to assert its influence over his brain and send him fleeing from the danger he faced.

But he did not run from the challenge, he ran *into* the challenge with deep commitment—as if it was crucial for him to master what he set out to do that day. He was staking his "existence" on the necessity of climbing that mini Everest in his path.

This imperious desire to survive, shown by so many warriors in their lives, in their careers, and in their sports endeavors, is the "Survivor's Imperative." It isn't a simple interest in succeeding because you and I know that is a tenuous position in the face of falling thirty-four times or having your land threatened by an attacking king. No one in his right mind would stand tall just to win.

No. This is much more a conviction. A deep-seated desire to survive in the face of nearly insurmountable adversity. The Spartan Survivor's Imperative was no different from the skateboarder's Survivor's Imperative because, to both groups, it was a will to survive that kept them going.

This is the commencement of the Excellence Ethos—choosing, out of a critical need to survive, to stand tall against all odds. Once an athlete, a student, or an employee has invoked the Survivor's Imperative, the choice for self-discovery and unimaginable growth has been opened. There is no turning back at that point. The journey will be tough and this challenge shapes you. It is not what you get when you arrive; it is what you become along the way that matters.

This is the power in that word *if.* It gave the Spartans the authority to survive as a people even when extinction seemed imminent. It provided the skateboarder with an urgency to master the trick, even when pain and failure were so prevalent.

As leaders, it should be our hope to plant the seeds of Survivor's Imperative in those we lead, so we can join them on their journey to excellence.

The Power of Language

Human language is a confusing construct. We have words with multiple meanings, words that convey entire thought processes, and entire sentences needed to define a single object. The orthography of most languages is deep and complex. Languages weren't developed in a lab under careful scrutiny but simply evolved over millennia at the whim of the speakers.

This causes the depth and richness of a language, the borrowing of words from other cultures, the combination of roots from multiple ancient peoples to form a word that conveys new meaning, and the development of phrases to account for cultural phenomena. Not to mention we add new words to a language each year based on the ever-evolving world in which we live. Imagine someone from the 1800s hearing us say, "I googled it." Oh, the confusion!

The complexity of our orthography is also affected by grammatical "rules" and the social constructs of different regions. I have to quote rules, as there is no such thing as a hard and fast rule in language, at least in English. The letter *I* does not always come before the letter *E*, except after *C*. They are suggestions. In addition, New Yorkers talk "to" you, but when I lived in North Carolina, many people talked "at" me. I would laugh at first, but I soon became intrigued with the way people communicated based on cultural milieu, regional preferences, and upbringing. Our language is simply amazing.

With all this confusion, no hard and fast rules, and words having multiple meanings based on sentence structure or context, no wonder we struggle to communicate effectively with each other daily. We make fun of our current president for his awful grasp of the nuance of our language, for instance. We make fun of him "bigly" (???), but he knows words. Lots of good words. He doesn't use them the way some of us might use them, or he doesn't vary the use of certain words to convey the same meaning as some of us. We are simply different in how we view, understand, and use language. This can cause a "huge" disconnect among people.

Within the United States, we have difficulty effectively communicating between regions. Have you ever heard a Bostonian try to carry on a long conversation with a person from the bayou? They may as well be speaking two different and unrelated languages. They aren't, and neither is incorrect in how the language is formed and employed. Imagine then, what it must be like for someone not from our country? Especially someone from a country with a simpler and more straightforward orthography, like Finland. How confusing it must be to see the word "lead" and know it is pronounced differently based on the sentence in which it is used. Or try to give the plural of deer or mouse. Shouldn't it be deers and mouses? Maybe it is meece?

Then they find out we park on driveways and drive on parkways. Simply put, language matters, but language is difficult. It is also a living, breathing "organism" that is subject to change, adaptation, and evolution based on a region, a dialect, a cultural upbringing, or environmental factors.

If our language, if our words more specifically, are so difficult among people, especially those who speak the same language, imagine what our words do within our brains? We are smart. We are intuitive. We have a "supercomputer" strapped to our shoulders—which, by the way, we are very good at catchphrases, analogies, metaphors, and onomatopoeias to also convey deeper meaning to our words. Using the word *supercomputer* is a great way to help people understand how the brain works. It was a brilliant metaphor, although one that is now being challenged in science—but I digress.

For as astute as we are, and for as powerful as our brains are, they are "computers" after all and run processes as computers would. They can basically be coded. Let's just run with that idea for a bit until it is fully debunked. It helps make my case here. With a computer, we code it to perform tasks. Based on what the code is, the tasks are completed. The brain ends up being coded by our thoughts and words, just like a computer. The process we need to go through to make coffee in the morning, for instance, is a series of steps. A code. When followed, it produces the same outcome: a cup of joe.

> **Words are the code of our brain, the software that helps the hardware achieve maximum potential.**

The one flaw within the coding process is that it is literal. The computer follows the steps. If something in the environment is altered, the computer follows the steps but may not get the same result. Everything is at face value. Many people talk about the "if this, then that" construct for running processes. If this happens, then that should happen. Simple enough, unless a condition is changed in the system, causing an error. In addition, if the human who has to input the data makes an error in the code, the result will also go haywire.

At its root, the brain processes. We are not artificially intelligent, and therefore, we account for human error, environment changes, and other extraneous variables that may affect the outcome of the code. We adapt intelligently and agilely to the tasks at hand. At its root, the brain is comprised of cells with neurons and synapses; a neuron fires and the synapse receives the signal. There is no accounting for environment or error at that level of firing. It fires and the "skill loop" is then complete.

For athletes, this means building the myelin sheath around the synapse to ensure it fires strongly and exactly each time. This is the rote definition of building skill; proper reps under game circumstances should yield a thicker myelin sheath, resulting in more effective completion of a skill.

So the thicker the sheath, the better. The more we do something exactly the same each time, the thicker the sheath becomes. Practice makes perfect.

What does this have to do with the price of tea in China (a colloquialism showing, again, how strange language is)? Not only do physical skills process in this manner, but words also process similarly. The more we read, the more we enrich the neuron pathways in the brain and "build a bigger brain." Research has shown households where parents read to their children and use more advanced words, as well as speak to them often, tend to have children with brains that grow faster and more effectively. It is why schools beg us to read to our children at night. We are forging neural pathways every time we speak to them.

My wife is a prime example of someone who was exposed to such an environment. There was a lot of reading and dialogue in her home growing up. Her parents also spoke in larger words and varied the vocabulary, exposing her to a dictionary of terms and phrases. She and I are both language geeks, and we love carrying on conversations that further expand our minds and vocabulary. We try to insert new words that hold the same meaning instead of sharing everyday words we get into the habit of using. We try to stump each other. It is a fun game and a wonderful learning experience.

She jokes about how she used to nanny for a couple, one who had a PhD in "rocket science" and one with an MBA from a well-respected Ivy League school. They both used to ask her to repeat and define words she would use. They would quip about her huge vocabulary and marvel at the words she knew.

She used to say, "How is it that my vocabulary is bigger than theirs?"

Neural pathways. She built more around language. That's where her myelin sheath is thicker. I am sure the MBA, who is also one of the top international mergers and acquisitions executives in the country, has a better grasp of financial models than my wife, and certainly, the "rocket scientist" understands the dynamics of flow a bit better than her. That's how and where they built their thick myelin sheaths.

So words build the brain. But words also code the brain. They imprint memories, processes, feelings, and behaviors on our brains. When we hear words, they cause emotional, physical, and psychological reactions that drive thoughts and behaviors. There are reactions that occur deep in our brains without our need to "think" about them because they have been coded already. They are "instinctual" reactions. More likely, they are rote, or automatic, like the software code running as it always does.

If this is the case, then when we speak to others, or even to ourselves, our brains hear words and then run processes based on the words that are heard. We do not have to think about it; we do not have to give any input, but that also means we do not affect the outcome. It is like code in software. It simply runs without regard for environment or error.

See where I am going with all of this?

We need to understand the awesome power of words and the interaction of our brains with words. Four things can happen when words are "spoken."

First, words trigger visceral reactions. Some words are attached to specific moments, emotions, and behaviors. We hear the word and our brains have an immediate reaction. Sights, sounds, smells, and emotions flood back swiftly.

"Stop!"

I don't have to think about that word. It somehow imprinted itself onto my brain during a very emotional and dramatic moment in my life and triggers an immediate visceral response.

"Stop" halts me in my tracks, causes an adrenaline spike that is attached to an emotion, alerts my senses to the surroundings, and shuts out other processes. I instinctually stop, look, and listen. "Stop" was used when I was doing something I shouldn't have and could've gotten hurt, like running into traffic or climbing on the shelves at the grocery store. My mom would scream that word, "Stop!" When I hear it now, I immediately return to those moments. I can hear the traffic, see Mom's face, and understand the fear in her eyes. It's all triggered by that single word, and my brain reacts without any input from me.

Second, the brain does not distinguish between who is saying the word or the "reality" of it being stated. In other words, whether I use a word or someone else uses it, the brain simply processes the word. It also cannot distinguish between the word being thought by me or spoken to me by someone else. Words are words; they do not only exist in our realities but also the virtual realms of our brains. Words are in our thoughts, in our dreams, in our speech, and in our "imagery." The brain has no idea where the words come from. It simply carries out the command to react, just like a computer does. It doesn't matter who typed the word.

"Can't"

The brain identifies, defines, and synthesizes the word. It makes no difference if it was said by another person or if it was thought by you. The moment *can't* is heard, the brain processes it. Too late. *Can't* triggers a failure mechanism in us, a fear reaction.

Can't tells our brain to consider the negative outcome if we try and fail. Would we be embarrassed, get hurt, get into trouble, or succeed? It is weighing the odds of success now and looking for an "escape route."

This word raises doubt, creates cautiousness and concern, lowers our confidence, and casts a shadow of negativity.

What we were once excited to achieve or thought was attainable is now under serious doubt-filled scrutiny. Should we try? Is it better to gracefully bow out before disaster? What if the consequences of failure far outweigh the reward?

Can't is a powerful word that triggers a fixed mindset reaction and causes our amygdala to assert its opinion: "Hey, man, I think we should either fight this or run . . . but do something fast before this gets bad." Athletes who play with *can't* imprinted on their brains are either tentative, anxious, and fearful or aggressive, anxious, and fearful. The "lizard brain"—the non-rational, primitive part of the brain—causes us to go "red head" (as the New Zealand All Blacks rugby team would say) and lose our focus and any control of our emotions.

Can't is not the only word that can trigger these kinds of emotions, but you can see how powerful a word can be and how the brain does not distinguish between who said it. Once the word *can't* is uttered, the brain simply reacts.

Third, words can cause a filter effect using "if this then that." Perhaps we've heard a word so many times in our lives that our brains become numb to the word. Or trial and error proved that word to be ineffective, and thus, the brain now filters it, rendering it obsolete.

"Don't"

Our brain reacts to *don't* because it was heard two trillion times a day growing up, almost habitually, from those around us. *Don't* pull the dog's tail; *don't* touch the stove; *don't* dump out your milk, and *don't* poke your brother in the back seat of the car.

When we hear it now, we react in one of two ways: we focus on the negative, similar to *stop* and *can't*, and it shuts us down. Coaches who use *don't* tend to create players who are risk-averse, cautious, or even seize up in high-anxiety moments. They react as if they are touching a hot stove. "Red head" rules the day.

The other thing *don't* does is cause a filter effect. We were told *don't* when we jump three chairs into the pool, but it worked. We were told *don't* cross our eyes because they will stick that way, but they didn't. We were told don't stuff ten saltines at a time into our mouths because we would choke, but we didn't. So our brains see a trend. They filter *don't*. Our minds became a sieve for the word *don't* and let all the other words pass except for that one.

Bob Rotella, a world-renowned sports psychologist, said in *Golf is Not a Game of Perfect*, that the brain will drop "don't" from a sentence when used in high-anxiety situations.

Imagine you are standing on the 18th tee with a water hazard to your right but plenty of fairway to the left. Right before you swing, your last thought is, "Don't hit it in the water."

Bob believes your brain filters *don't* because it is numb to it. It simply does not hear the "don't" and only hears, "hit it in the water." That was the last thing you heard, and therefore, you hit the ball in the water.

Of course, if you are me, you know all your hits go right so dramatically that they need a turn signal. I hit it in the water and wonder if I used the phrase "Don't hit it in the water" or if my slice got the best of me again!

Can you recall a time this happened to you or to an athlete you coached? Your best shooter was up for the final penalty kick, and you gave the advice of "Don't miss."

Then she missed! Telling her *don't* caused "red head" to rule the day. She was anxious, felt the pressure, became cautious, tightened up, and missed. Her brain may have also acted as a sieve and only heard, "Miss."

Fourth, certain words simply trigger a series of psychosocial and physical reactions based on our experiences. The neural pathways were built over time by the use of those words, so our brains can quickly and easily access those pathways with one simple word. A sort of priming trigger or fast recall method.

Typically, these are words imprinted from an early age, when our brains are most laden with neurons and neural pathways (three billion at one point) and begin expanding or pruning based on usage. The more we hear a word, the more that pathway expands.

The pathways certain words imprint are very large, wide, fast neural networks. Like a superhighway, based on how often the word is used. The brain reacts more effectively and swiftly when a word is used more often. It becomes "automatic."

"Ghost"

Starting at age four, we would play "ghost in the graveyard" at our swim club. After swim meets, the parents would all sit around and talk at the pool, and we kids would go play in the large field or even the parking lot using the cars as "gravestones" for hiding (yes, we weren't thinking that one through). On the big family camping weekends at the swim club, which was nearly every weekend, all of us kids who were camping with our families would play in the big field at the back of the swim club near the campground. There were just enough trees to make it fun, and the tents served as hiding spots. Again, the parents did their thing, and we did ours.

When someone found the ghost, he or she would scream "Ghost!" and everyone tried to get back to home base before being tagged.

I heard that word—ghost!—a thousand times a summer for nearly fourteen years. It got to the point that my brain had a very wide, well-paved, and smooth neural pathway for a series of movements attached to the word. *Ghost* meant we should identify the location of the sound, turn from that location, duck down, and run as fast as possible to the base.

We didn't even think about it. We simply reacted and followed that sequence of actions automatically, every step run by our brain. This happens to athletes who have sported their entire lives to the sound of a gun, whistle, or bell. Hear the sound; the race begins. All those steps it took to teach the athlete to start fast—fire the arm forward, drive the back foot outward and into the ground, stay low, look at the finish line, arms in an *L* shape, etc.

Coaches painstakingly teach potential NFL players the perfect start to the forty-yard dash to get the fastest times. A great start could be the difference in millions of dollars. Every step and action is choreographed. They work for months on each motion, fine-tuning every element. The day arrives, and the gun goes off . . . and everything after that is automatic. The athlete swiftly and easily goes through the motions without thinking.

Words hold power. Words cause peril. They have an immediate, imperceptible, and uncontrollable effect on our brains. The moment they are spoken or thought, a process or series of processes are triggered in our brains. Emotions are brought up, reactions are created, senses are elevated, body changes are caused, and steps are taken.

How we react to those words depends on our environmental experiences with them. What happens when the word is said depends on how we have been trained over the years by the usage of the word.

Make no mistake. The impact of words is profound and simple all at once. Words lead to thoughts that lead to beliefs that lead to behaviors that become our reality. It sounds like new science or mumbo jumbo speak, but it is simply the way it is. Words are the binary code that runs the processes of our athletes' brains. It either turns the brain on to success or turns the brain off to failure.

My goal is to help you understand we have *full* control over the effect the words have on our athletes' brains if we are willing to be more intentional with them. If we are willing to eliminate some words, add new words, attach words to positive behaviors, and speak more consciously to our athletes, we can create even better performances. All with words.

In this book, we will discover the words of peril that should be eliminated from our vocabulary. We will discuss the words of power that can be used to create success, and we will identify the words we can use to help shape strong warrior mindsets and trigger success responses from our athletes. Ready? Set? Go! (More automatic action-producing words).

SECTION 2

Words and the Brain—
Installing the Right Software
for Peak Performance

Chapter 3

How the Brain Processes Words

Educators, coaches, parents, mentors, and other leaders must be aware of what and how they say things to those they lead.

Please forgive the nerd in me, but I want to take a little time to explain how words are both processed by and affect the brain.

The more we understand the simple science behind the factors that make us better leaders and coaches, the better we can be at developing effective strategies for employing these factors successfully in our daily actions. Knowing the technical aspects of words allows us to better provide tactical usages, mirroring skill development.

In other words, when I explain a skill to you, I am providing the *what*. My job is then to teach you the *how*, the learning of the technical skill. A technical skill learned in a vacuum is not useful unless I provide you with a context for the application. When you apply the skill to a game situation, it is the *why*, *when*, and *where*. A great coach always provides all of the aforementioned: what, how, why, when, and where.

Let's use an example here. What if your coach had only taught you to play your sport by talking about it? She simply defined new skills, explained how they worked, and then told you to accomplish learning the skills. No demonstration, no visual context, no step-by-step examples. How easy would it be to learn the skills, to adapt and grow?

I would suppose it would not be very easy for you. You would become frustrated in a short time and possibly give up on the skill. This is why most coaches find a way to demonstrate a skill. They provide visual cues, which are as important as verbal cues for learning the skill. We can easily mimic what we see and have explained to us.

In addition, visual cues cut down on the amount of time it takes to teach something. My wife was a group fitness teacher for years. She didn't just stand in front of the room and bark out what to do. That would have taken way too long to explain, step by step, how to perform the complex movement patterns she used in her classes. Instead, she stood in front of the room, with a wall of mirrors, and "demonstrated" the moves, while calling out the names. She was short-cutting the process of teaching and learning the moves.

For me to tell you all the amazing ways you can harness the power of certain words or avoid the peril of others but not explain how the brain actually processes and reacts to words would be counterintuitive to the coaching process. I am telling you the *what*, but you will have a better understanding of it and use it more effectively if I also show you the *how*.

Speech or language, or simply words, are merely environmental inputs to the brain, just as sights, smells, and the like. The brain receives the input stimulus and then processes it. This is a very simple explanation of the complex process the brain goes through to understand and comprehend words, but it shows the amount of work necessary for the brain to do so. Knowing this makes us understand how deeply words affect the brain and how much more effective we are when our words are aligned with what our desired outcomes are. Words that contradict or confuse what we are doing or wanting can delay success in our athletes.

The basic process for a spoken word in our brain follows a distinct path. Words are sounds that enter the ear; the sound waves are picked up in the inner ear and converted to nerve impulses. The nerve impulses travel along the auditory nerve to the auditory cortex. Those sounds are processed in the auditory cortex into words, distinguishing them from birds cawing, train horns honking, or the thump of a soccer ball. It doesn't stop there, though.

For words to be comprehended, there are two parts of the brain that help the auditory cortex process them. The first part of the brain to help is Wernicke's area, named for Carl Wernicke, who discovered it in 1874. This part of the brain lies in the posterior third of the brain, in the left hemisphere. It is abutting and behind the auditory cortex of the brain (makes sense to me for it to be close to the auditory cortex).

This section of the brain is important for the comprehension of speech sounds, thus it is the language comprehension area. It distills what we hear into coherent and understandable "thoughts." When words are spoken, the "message" is sent to Brodmann area 41 in the brain (the auditory complex). The words are then comprehended by Wernicke's area where the brain seems to contain "sound images" of those words (the visual component), and the word can then be comprehended by the brain. You speak; I process; I understand what was just said to me.

Think about a word and notice a visual will pop up in your mind. If I say lake, you get an actual mental image of a lake. Maybe it's one you visited, one you saw in a picture, or a lake you remember from a movie. You "see" the lake, and comprehension is much easier.

Wernicke's area is believed to help make that comprehension collection. People who have damage to Wernicke's area tend to struggle to comprehend spoken language. Their speech is typically fluent but empty of real content, or they talk in circles without ever conveying a complete thought. Comprehension is nearly impossible without Wernicke's area.

This is important to us for three reasons. First, we now know that what we say draws images in the mind to whom we are speaking. This is vital to realize that we imprint on the brain with every word spoken. If our physical actions differ from what is spoken, it only serves to confuse someone who has a different picture in his or her head.

Second, simply because someone is hearing what we say does not mean they are comprehending what we say. Or, as I always tell coaches with whom I work, "Just because you coached it, it doesn't necessarily mean they learned it."

Worse, they may have comprehended and interpreted what you said in a completely different manner than what you expected. Simply because you said something and understand it to have a certain meaning in your mind, it does not necessitate they have the same meaning in their minds. Your comment could be as simple as, "If you win tomorrow, we will have practice the following day." You could simply mean you expect them to win, but since you cannot predict the future, you shouldn't count your chickens until they hatch. You are superstitious and don't want to jinx it.

Your athletes, on the other hand, may have comprehended that their coach is uncertain because he doesn't have faith in them, or he thinks the other team is better. *If* is a vague word, creating peril. They comprehended it differently. Parlaying any jinx was not even a possibility in their comprehension and interpretation of the sentence. All because of that darned word, *if.*

Third, words, beliefs, and actions need to be aligned for us to be effective communicators with our athletes. You may say something to your athletes, but if you are acting differently or believe differently, the comprehension will be thrown off by it.

> **Just because you coached it, it doesn't necessarily mean they learned it.**

I sometimes experiment with coaches. I will teach a group of players a new move. I will tell them I want them to "roll the ball forward with their left foot and then push it to the side with the outside of the same foot." Then I demonstrate the move by "pulling" the ball back with my right foot and pushing it to the outside.

Two different moves, and my explanation differs from my demonstration. Typically, the athletes stare at me. Some may be brave enough to call me out for being confusing. Most try the move but fail because the visual didn't match the words. The visual I created in their brain will roll and the left foot was not what they saw. Their brain image is not a match, and therefore, it slows the learning process down. Comprehension went sideways. Sometimes, interchanging a simple word like *roll* instead of *pull* will cause the same effect.

What if my tone was more of a question than a statement of fact? Would that also confuse comprehension?

Imagine I say to my players, "You are the masters of your own destiny?" in a questioning, soft tone, where my voice rises at the end of the sentence. As if I was asking them whether they were the masters of their own destinies or implying I didn't believe they could master their own destinies. What would be the comprehension of that sentence and the subsequent sound image formed in their brain? They would most likely jog slowly onto the field, unsure of the amount of control they had.

If I shouted it, with a clenched fist, a full voice, and a look of confidence, ending with a knowing nod at them, how then would they interpret it? They'd probably take the field at a sprint, ready to tear apart anything in their way.

Comprehension also happens in the delivery. Those sounds have an impact on the brain in vastly different ways and lend to more accurate and effective comprehension. Clarity, alignment, conviction, and expectations matter to what we say because Wernicke's area will comprehend words based on the sound image attached.

A second area of the brain that assists with speech processing is Broca's area. It's set in the anterior third of the brain in the left hemisphere, to the front of and abutting the auditory complex (anterior frontal gyrus). It is named for the French neurologist, Paul Broca, who discovered it in 1861. He asserted that patients who had damage to the anterior frontal gyrus had difficulty or disruptions to speech production.

For many years, it was thought speech production was the only thing Broca's area was responsible for, but in recent years, research has shown patients with lesions to Broca's area also cannot use syntactical information to form comprehension of spoken language. They cannot determine the meaning of sentences based on the placement and types of the words (syntax).

For instance, if I said, "John brommed the ball," you could at least use syntactic information to glean some meaning from the sentence. You know that brommed is placed between "John" and "ball," you might infer that John is the agent and the ball is the object. "Brommed" would therefore seem to be a verb, so John took some kind of action on the ball.

Imagine not being able to use syntax for comprehension? We have a complex language as it is; syntax helps us at least break down some of the complexity.

Broca's area and Wernicke's area are connected by a bundle of nerves called the arcuate fasciculus. This seems to help coordinate processing between the two areas. People with damage to this bundle can understand spoken language but cannot form comprehensible sentences and cannot repeat words spoken to them. We are more interested in how we process, interpret, and react to words, but you can see the complexity of the auditory complex within our brains.

The takeaway here is this: words, once spoken, cause sound images and are placed into "context" by the two areas assisting our auditory complex. Our tone, pitch, body language, actions, and even the placement of the word within a sentence will affect how our teammates interpret and react to the word. All this from a simple sound entering the ear!

Speak It. Think It. Do It.

One final thought on words: If our brains are like computers, then words are the code that runs the computers. The words tell our brains what processes need to happen to function. They enter our brains as sounds and then become the software for our lives.

What is spoken to us is then processed as thought and finally executed as action. This is the Occam's Razor explanation for what words do to our brains. Simply put, speak it; think it; do it. A computer with no code executes no commands. Once we add code, it will then do exactly as we say. That's why computer experts proclaim, "It was user error." The computer is incapable of an error because the code in the computer was not created by the computer but by a human. Even the most adept AI, if it were to malfunction, would inform us, "It can only be contributed to human error." We told it what to do, and it did exactly as we said. It cannot deviate from the script. It must execute what is said to it.

If our brains are to be viewed as computers with extremely advanced AIs, then what is said to us and what we think become the code that runs the hardware. Though we have free will and the intelligence to analyze, synthesize, and create thought, the code of our words still leaves an imprint. More times than expected, our brains simply do as the code says.

It's not only spoken words but their thoughts that matter. Words are words to the brain, whether they came from someone else or originated from that "voice" within the mind. When we speak to those who trust in and count on us, what we say will also become their inner voice. Our words echo. Repeated again, the brain embeds that code deeper and deeper into automaticity.

This automaticity is vital in performance-based situations. As anxiety rises, pressure mounts, and activity seems to speed up on us in those moments of "high-performance," and our brains will rely on shortcuts and easily retrieved functions. It will go into a survive-or-thrive mode, depending on how well prepared, physically and psychologically, we are for the moment. The brain will go into automatic mode. The processes will run in the background, affecting our performance, without us having any knowledge it is happening. Just as our computer carries out multitudes of functions without us needing to input them each time (it's already installed), our brains will do the same.

Speak it. Think it. Do it.

Educators, coaches, parents, mentors, and other leaders must be aware of what and how they say things to those they lead. As someone in any of these roles, you have the choice to install malware or beautiful software in their brains. Words that become code that will put the brain on autopilot for executing certain functions. What code do you want to install?

In addition, when working with your teams, you must be acutely aware of the "pre-installed" software. Others have come before you and written their own codes. Your team members have used their voices and, thus, written an internal code. Layer upon layer of code has been written over the years by parents, friends, bullies, coaches, and even the person's own voice. You cannot assume they are a blank slate. You must be aware of the fact you may have to undo some malware, deal with previously ingrained automaticity, and more. This means you need to exercise a little patience, empathy, and grace.

It also means the hardware of your athletes will only be able to perform at the level of the software. Have you ever had a computer that was supposed to be the fastest, most efficient one on the market, but you inadvertently downloaded something onto it? What happened to it? Did it still function at peak performance?

Not likely. The hardware performance, no matter how well built it was, became hindered by the software trying to run it. Athletes are potentially similar in this aspect. They could have won the genetic lottery from a physical ability standpoint and could have been trained to be technically dominant, and yet, if they have a destructive internal voice or have lost confidence because of the voices of others, they simply may not perform at peak. The software will limit the performance of the hardware.

Most coaches call that a "bad day" or say, "She can't handle the pressure," or call it "a choke." It's funny how we say that about an athlete trying to perform in a very dynamic and challenging physical, mental, and emotional environment, and yet, nobody ever says, "Dang, my computer is pulling a total choke job during this presentation today" in the business world. We might say, "I seem to have a software issue." Athletes can have those too.

This book will reveal the various words that act as triggers for sets of commands already installed in our brains. It will show us the stories of how those words have either enhanced performance (power words) or limited performance (peril words) as they set off a series of processes in the brain once uttered or thought.

We must help those we lead by not only using power words that will help them unlock peak performance but also by guiding them with the proper words, teaching them to speak to themselves in ways that unlock their best performance, and giving them the tools to install the software that supports the brain.

SECTION 3

Power Words—Words that Enhance Peak Performance

Chapter 4

Go

———◆———

Words have the power to draw us back to distant memories from childhood and then connect those experiences with an entirely new generation.

Go. The word would echo across the empty pool deck and hang in the valley where our swim club was located. During these early summer morning practices, in a small valley about 200 yards off the road and behind the still houses, our coaches calling out our starts were the only sounds one could hear.

This is how we began all practices. It is also how we began all meets. We would stand in lines behind our assigned lanes, grouped by age, and wait for the start. Once every swimmer was ready (the older, the more serious, or the more astute had to put on their caps and goggles), the coaches would start us. Not with a whistle or a beep but with the simple word "go."

They'd call it out, and the first swimmers in each lane dove in, the next in line stepping up for their turn. It began as a joke when I was very small because the water felt so cold and uninviting on those early summer mornings. All our schoolmates were still sleeping, and here we were prepping to jump into freezing water. The mere thought of it paralyzed most of us.

Swimmers slept on the chairs under towels; some hid in the bathrooms, and others would perch on the edge staring pathetically at the still waters. Once we did get in, no one would actually swim, we would jump about in the water complaining and screaming.

One day, our coach told us we would just dive in from the deep end and get it over with instead of slowly peeling off the Band-Aid. So we were lined up by age in different lanes, assigned to us forevermore, and when he called, "Go!" we dove in and started swimming. He said we would dive right in and get to work. Once we heard the word, it was time for business. We were fighting tunas, and when we hit that water, it was fighting time.

The word *go* became a tradition after that day. Years later, still following tradition, the word did not simply represent the ripping off of the Band-Aid on cold mornings at the pool. It was representative of so much more.

It became our call to action. It was the first thing we heard in the morning and the first thing we heard when we assembled for battle at meets. The word *go* meant it was time to get serious. It was time to go to war. The word itself would rend us from any sleepy stupor or psychological quagmire (as many teens are prone to having) and send us off into the water, ready to compete.

Those of us who had been there since the first time we heard the word had a special kinship with it and with each other. It was much like the horns that signified the start of battles. When we heard the word, it triggered us into "work" mode.

I don't know if it was out of habit or simply by accident, but I caught myself, years later, when I was a coach saying, "Go!" to my athletes when it was time to take the soccer field. At first, I would run teams through their pre-game routines using *go* as the start word. I would meticulously explain to each team I coached the sideline represented the line between their non-soccer life and their soccer life. The moment they crossed that line, they would leave everything they brought to the game that did not pertain to soccer on the other side. It was their trigger to let go of school worries, relationship worries, homework issues, or anything else that weighed on their minds. It was "go time."

By the end of my career, I no longer even ran pre-game routines. My teams followed their own rituals and had their own habits of excellence that guided their pre-game process. I showed up, set up for them, and once they had all assembled, one of the leaders would simply call out, "Go!" Game day began, their job started, and I would sit back and enjoy it.

I even had captains who mimicked me and said, "It's go time." This brought the group to an entirely new level. A captain would state it, the team would all step onto the field, and it was as if they were different people—like little warriors ready to stand by each other until the final whistle. The battle cry had been sounded, and the hounds had been released.

This is the power of one word. Words have the power to draw me back to distant memories from my childhood and then connect those experiences with an entirely new generation. To instantly change our demeanor from one of resistance, sluggishness, or chaos and plunge us deep into the flow of the athlete's mindset. Of course, we hadn't cornered the market on this concept. Teams the world over, even the fictional ones, used a similar tactic to prep.

On *Friday Night Lights*, Coach Taylor compelled his players in the doorway of the locker room with, "Clear eyes, pure heart, can't lose,"[2] and then they would storm the field, ready. The Haka, famously performed by the New Zealand All Blacks, readies the men for their battle. The Haka calls up their ancestors to go into battle with them; it clears their heads, readies their hearts, and calls the legacy forth to remind them of what they came to do.

They say the Haka is one of the most intimidating moments in all of sport. To see these massive men of great power and part of a legacy of champions for over one hundred years standing before you, screaming at the top of their lungs . . . to know they are calling upon the legacy of champions, clearing their minds so only one thought remains—battle— is intimidating. Opponents know they will battle until they win or run out of time. That takes the "go" call to an entirely new level of excellence.

Trigger words like this are ways to clear the mechanism, a strategy for garnering as much focus as possible. In the movie *For Love of the Game*, Kevin Costner (his character was named Chapel) is standing on the pitcher's mound but is distracted by the thousands of fans in the stadium around him. Horns are blowing, fans are deriding him, and the cacophony is unbearable. Chapel looks around the stadium for a moment and then says to himself, "Clear the mechanism." A passing train goes from loud to nearly silent and all background noise nearly disappears, like turning on the noise canceling feature on one's headphones. The fans are still screaming, but he can no longer hear them.

Chapel looks toward the batter and says, "Hello, Mike." When the camera pans out, the background is blurred and only the sixty feet, six inches between Chapel and the batter is shown clearly. Only the task at hand is relevant in the mechanism (his mind). Then, the moviegoer hears the ball hit the catcher's glove, and the umpire calls out, "Strike one!"

Trigger words can shut out all that is happening in the environment, all those extraneous stimuli that will only confuse, diffuse, or refuse the psyche. We did it as local swim league athletes and the All Blacks did it as some of the greatest athletes on the planet. It pervades the pre-game or pre-shot routine of nearly all high-level athletes. Some may not even realize they are doing it!

Have you ever seen the pre-game walks of basketball players, football players, or soccer players when they arrive at the stadium hours before game time? They saunter off the team bus, headphones on, hoodies up, and heads nodding to the music—some not even noticing the people around them. Many listen to the same song for every game, out of tradition or superstition, but the effect is a clearing of the mechanism like what happened in *For Love of the Game*.

Baseball players have a batting song. The stadium plays it as they walk out to the plate. Do you think that may trigger them, prime them to compete? It sure does. The song causes a series of processes in the brain. Memories of big hits are called to mind, and there may be images of the ball slowing down so they can see it. They smell the fresh-cut grass in the outfield from one hundred yards away, feel the bat vibrate in their hands, and hear the loud crack of the leather ball on wood. *Then,* they step up to the plate with the mechanism of the world around them on mute and only one thing in clear focus: that ball sixty feet away that will soon be hurtling at them at ninety miles per hour.

There is great power in a word or string of words that can clear the mechanism and prepare athletes to compete. As coaches, we should be seeking those moments or words that can be used to help our athletes "center themselves," "clear the mechanism," or get into "the flow." There are practical and easy ways to do this with your team, regardless of level or age.

Namely, help them create pre-game or pre-shot routines. If you work with your athletes to create routines that they use each time they perform, those routines become habits. They will do them automatically, and they will also become opportunities for them to embed the moment in their brains and forget the stressors, relieve the pressure, and clear their minds. With those routines, help your athletes use words that set the tone. Just like "Go!" was our trigger word to let us know it was "game time" or how Coach Taylor called his players with "clear eyes, full heart, can't lose."

> **Words can ignite and incite. Having a trigger word for peak performance ignites the competitive fire and incites confidence. Go find your trigger word.**

Encourage athletes to create their own language. At first, this may seem like an inane idea, but all great cultures invent a language. When I work with groups using my Warriors Not Winners program, the words I use are taken directly from some of the greatest warrior-athlete cultures that have ever existed. These words make no sense to my clients, at first. They seem like weird phrases or gibberish, but as the program unfolds and we connect those words to the mission of the culture, the shared values, and the legacy of the team, the words take on great meaning. Great cultures have inside jokes; they have catchphrases, and they have mantras, which they share only with each other. If you are encouraging your team to invent a language, you are in the bonus; not only are they developing "go" words and other words in the language of excellence, but they are also bonding as a team. You're building an intentional culture.

Take time in your training to teach your athletes how to reset themselves mid-performance too. All athletes struggle with mental lapses during pressure situations, but young ones tend not to have the skills or resources necessary to recover. One mistake sets the mind reeling a bit. Focus is lost, outside stimuli assert an influence, more mistakes are made, and the fragile balance or flow state is lost to a spiraling, out-of-control mindset. Great athletes have learned to recover.

Like in a video game, they can learn to hit the reset button and start the game over with a fresh set of lives. Young athletes can be trained to do this, and it usually starts with the clearing of the mechanism. Shutting down negative self-talk, shutting out the crowd, turning off the racing mind, and starting over fresh. A great reset button, as I call it with my athletes, typically has to do with "triggering the mind" to a calmer state, slowing down, and employing a physical movement pattern that grounds the athlete . . . and, of course, a word.

We see this with free throw shooters, batters, and golfers on the tee box. Some have been known to tap their club or kick their spikes an exact number of times, say something to themselves, close their eyes for a moment, take a deep breath, and then be ready. This is a pre-shot routine, but it is also a calming mechanism. The All Blacks train as much on the software of great athletes as they do the hardware. They are as focused on the mental state, emotional skills, and mindfulness of their players as they are on the weight room and the skills training. They talk about not having a "red head" in competition, which equates to being stressed, out of control, and emotional. It is akin to the fight-or-flight response welling up from the amygdala, and no one can fully control emotions and psychological processes in this state. They work to keep a "blue head" of control: intentionality, mindfulness, and staying "present."

Richie McCaw, the former All Blacks heroic captain, could be seen stamping his feet firmly on the ground and saying a mantra to himself when he started to feel the red head coming. This is how he grounded himself in the moment to maintain control. It was his reset button.

For young athletes, it may take you looking them in the eyes in the beginning. Connection is key for young kids, and eye-to-eye contact will not only create the connection but provide a conduit for you to transfer your calm, allowing them a safe space for calming down and centering. During this time, teach them a word to clear the mechanism. It could be as simple as "breathe" or as meaningful as a team motto—something that connects them emotionally and psychologically to calmness and control and allows them to reset "fresh." Words are amazing reset buttons when used by coaches.

Spend time teaching your athletes values. Tell moral stories or fables often to teach them the cultural values and lessons that matter. Children love stories, and they remember them more than if we simply speak directions or instructions to them. In these stories, you can embed the values of the team, the mission of the organization, and the life lessons you wish to teach. The byproduct is that the words you use become their words too. They begin repeating the stories and the phrases with each other in game situations. Those words become the anchors to the moment and the battle cries of the team.

I had a handful of phrases I used often as a coach. I never realized how much those became the language of excellence for my players until years later, they would repeat them to me, or I would catch one of my former players using them in his coaching. I even saw the parents of my kids putting those words in picture books and on shirts. Those words became the cultural language, the triggers, the reset buttons, and the "clear the mechanism" words that worked.

Such a phrase in my time working with athletes was "Bring it in." One of the last teams I ever coached used "Bring it in" as their way to clear the mechanism. When I held out my arms for the pregame huddle—where we all linked arms over shoulders—and I said, "Bring it in," the boys knew it was the final moment before they took the field. It was "go time," and it was now or never. They were twelve years old, and it still triggered a competitive spirit in each of them. Age and level do not matter if we are consistent with our words and create a language of excellence to help our athletes "clear the mechanism."

Chapter 5

When

Coaches and athletes who speak with when statements are
bolstering confidence and creating growth mindsets.

The year was 2012. I was enrolled in a Master's of Education program
and immersed in the student teaching process. I had been assigned to a
first-grade classroom with Ms. G. She was one of my all-time favorite
teachers, and I didn't even have her as a teacher. She was an amazing
mentor.

She taught me things like, "You can lighten up but you can never
tighten up," for instilling a sense of discipline, focus, and order at the
beginning of the year. We worked an entire morning with the students
on recognizing where each child's name was in the alphabetical order list
and lining up in that order. We then marched through the halls multiple

times until we had the order and the process down to a science. Our children were focused and disciplined.

She also taught me about connecting with the children, engaging them in ways that empowered them to think for themselves, holding each other accountable, and what it means to teach the person, not the desk. She cared deeply about each child, and they loved her.

I learned so much from Ms. G.—too much to recount here. She was a master mentor and an amazing human. One of the greatest lessons I ever learned from her, she didn't even know she was teaching me.

A young boy in our class had fallen ill years before of a very rare cancer in his brain. He had been in remission and doing very well, but from the very first day of class, we were on high alert, looking for symptoms. Ms. G. had taught the student's siblings and knew the family well. We had been well-trained in what to look for, and sadly, about midway through the year, he started showing strange mannerisms.

Ms. G. noticed immediately and notified the parents. Something was off, and she was not taking chances. She was right. His condition had returned, and he was sent to the hospital. We did not see for him days. We were kept apprised of his condition, but everyone was concerned.

The nation's top specialist for his condition was in the same city, so he had the best care, but everyone worried that the second time around would not be as easy on him. There was a good chance it would be his last year with us.

I knew a collegiate hockey goalie who had founded a children's charity. He invited kids to his games and visited them in the hospital. I knew this would be such a boost in morale for our student and his classmates. I arranged for a visit to the classroom once the boy had been released from the hospital and was ready to return to school—albeit slowly.

It was an amazing day. The goalie visited with hockey sticks, pucks, and team spirit wear for the boy, as well as gifts for the entire class. The boy was surprised by the gesture, elated to meet the goalie. It was a boost for us all.

When they were taking pictures, the player leaned in and said, "If you get healthy enough, we can have you up for a game. How's that sound?"

Without missing a beat, Ms. G. firmly and calmly corrected him.

"*When* he is healthy, that will be an awesome night."

She didn't scold the player. It wasn't overbearing. It was a loving correction, a matter-of-fact rephrasing, and it was powerful. With one word change, she gave hope to a boy who had seen enough trauma and experienced enough fear and pain for a lifetime.

With that one word, *when,* she switched an unsure comment into a confident and real future. And it effectively shifted the beliefs of all of us from a foundation of uncertainty to one of certainty.

When Bolsters Confidence

I have never forgotten that lesson. Ms. G. didn't mean it as a lesson; she simply lived out who she was. Confident, certain, hopeful, and resilient. The children she taught were also confident and resilient. They never doubted their ability to learn or their skills because she was a futurist. She was someone who believed things would definitely happen, and that is a far more powerful way to view the world.

If is a peril word, but *when* is a word that bestows great power to both the speaker and the listener. It transmits strong confidence. It is not the kind of word that "fakes it 'til you make it," but it is a word that belies absolute confidence that something *will* happen.

Athletes who speak with *when* statements are bolstering confidence and creating growth mindsets. They move from vague dreams of what could be to a clear reality of what will happen next. In high-performance situations, when anxiety is rising and confidence is taking a beating, having clarity and confirmation of future success is key. When the game comes down to inches or seconds, having a firm hold on the few inches between your ears makes all the difference for competitors.

As leaders, we hold that irrefutable power to influence and bolster our charges' confidence by moving them into *when*-language scenarios. Like Ms. G, we can firmly and lovingly guide them to more confidence by simply changing the first word in their dreams or hopes.

> ***When* means "I believe," and there is no greater way to tap into a competitive fire than to believe something will be done.**

First, we must use *when* in our speech. When teaching skills or tactics, we should refer to "when you learn this" instead of copping to an "if you learn" mentality. Our willingness to use *when* during teaching shows our confidence in the athletes we lead and bolsters their self-confidence.

Second, when prepping them for competition, *when* statements create greater clarity around the outcome on the "battlefield." Many of us want to give our teams clear directions for the games, like a commander's intent. To do this, we should use *when* language to prescribe the exact way the game will look for us when all is said and done. This is not about wins and losses. It is about providing clarity about how they will play and guiding their expectations. Telling a team "when" as you describe the game strategy plants a powerful seed that will germinate throughout the game.

Third, firmly correct those athletes struggling with confidence. The easiest (but not productive) way for a player suffering from a lack of belief in their abilities to protect their ego is to use vague statements and weak promises. They want to say "if" to soften the blow of possible failure. Your job is to move them past the thought of failure to the idea of success with a "when" correction. "If I can learn to juggle five times" can be firmly, yet lovingly, changed by responding, "*When* you get there, imagine the excitement you will feel about working so hard and then experiencing the joy of having reached the goal." There's a reason cheesy movies exist; the language of success does work. The brain hears it loud and clear.

Finally, *when* gives athletes a reminder that, though this is a marathon and the magic is in the journey, there is a spot on the map. All athletes need to know about and see the end to have some hope of reaching it. When we drive with our children, they have no clue how long it will take or where we are going. This is confusing, scary, and boring as heck. When we give them landmarks, timelines, and images of what it will be like on arrival, they are much more pleased with the journey. Using *when* language gives our athletes something to "look forward to" and something for which to strive. However, be careful to get them back into closely monitoring their progress and not looking off to the horizon all of the time.

This is the power of *when*. A word that can bring out of the distant and unknown future, a very clear and attainable reality. A word that gave a little boy hope instead of fear and taught an old dog a new way of speaking to his athletes.

By the way, that boy is alive and healthy today. His smile and the lesson I learned stays with me, and the invaluable mentorship of Suzy G has helped me immensely in my career.

Chapter 6

You

*Shifting the power by using "you" has a
natural reward effect on people.*

We were at Satchel's Pizza in Gainesville, Florida, sharing dinner with a group of friends. One of our friends was a long-time childcare provider. She was brilliant with children. Not simply as a teacher or caregiver, but generally, she really connected with them, understood them, and communicated effectively with them. I was in awe every time I watched her interact with my kids. She was our youngest, Cameron's, caregiver, and we loved the person she was helping to shape in him. He adored her too.

On this particular night, we were deep in the throes of potty-training Cameron. "Popo," as she was affectionately called by all the children, had done a masterful job potty-training him during the day. We would drop him off with some changes of clothes and leave it all to her. In a week, she had him able to identify when he needed to go and get to the right place to do so. The only concern was he would relapse with us at home and on the weekends from time to time.

Here we were, eating in a very crowded public place, and Cameron jumps up from his seat and states he needs to go potty. My wife rushes him off to the bathroom. Several minutes later, he emerges from the bathroom with a flourish, sprints to the middle of the crowded pizza joint, and with a triumphantly loud voice, announces, "I pooped on the potty all by myself!"

There he is, standing in the middle of the restaurant now, arms outstretched, an ear-to-ear grin, having informed the entire place of his recent accomplishment. The place erupted in laughter and applause. Everyone was cheering on our son, who had let the world know he performed a normal, basic human function—in an eating establishment, nonetheless! Thank goodness they all saw the humor in it.

Popo was the first to speak to him when he arrived at the table. My wife was running after him with this amused look on her face but beaming with pride. Popo looked Cameron right in the eyes and said, "You must be very proud of yourself, Cameron!"

His little chest puffed up, he lifted his arms above his head, and yelled, "I am!"

I was awestruck. I studied Popo for a moment. Had she known exactly what she had done? Was she aware of the powerful implications of her words? She had to have known it. If not intentionally, from some scientific study, but from natural instinct developed over the years of working with children with such brilliant success, she had to have been aware of how powerful her words were at that moment.

Actually, it was one word that held so much power. One word that transferred power from us adults, namely Popo, to our son Cameron and empowered him to continue down the path he had started. It dawned on me, later and after some reflection, why he would lapse in his progress with us. When he was with Popo, he held power over his learning. She allowed him to have influence, whereas when he was with us, we held all of the power. We wanted him to go to the bathroom on our schedule; we wanted him to do it our way, and when he accomplished the task, we told him how proud *we* were of him. When he was with us, it was all about what we wanted, not what *he* wanted. He had no power or influence over the process, even though it was a deeply personal event.

At Popo's, he chose when he needed to go to the bathroom. He chose how he did it. Of course, she had the patience and ability to do this, and we didn't always have that luxury, but that was not the real genius in this lesson. The real genius of it all was that when he was successful in his endeavor, Popo gave him the power again with one simple word: *you.*

She did not say, "I am so proud of you," which maintains an adult's upper hand, keeps the ultimate influence with us, and robs him of feeling like he accomplished something. He was merely the pawn in our moment of successful teaching when we showed him how proud we were. As if we did all the work and should get all the credit. One simple word transferred that much power!

Popo was genius enough to tell him how proud *he* should feel about it. She reinforced that he did all the work, that he had all the influence over his learning, and that he deserved all the credit. The proof of the pudding is in the eating.

When he was being told how proud he should feel, he continued to progress with his learning. He had fewer and fewer accidents at her house. He could recognize earlier when he needed to go and get to the bathroom on time. Not only that, but he was more independent once he got to the bathroom.

At home, he still had a fair mix of accidents with successes, and he still acted dependent on us when he made it to the bathroom. At home, we held the power or influence over the learning. At Popo's, his learning had become self-directed. It was his choice, his pace, and his process.

Of course, we immediately shifted our words to match Popo's, and he potty-trained much faster than our other two. Could it be the result of having older siblings? Maybe. Could it have to do with the fact we changed "I" to "you" when we celebrated his successes? Yes.

You Must Be Proud of Yourself

I've since applied this technique in coaching, teaching, and child-rearing situations. It works. It shortens the learning curve; it empowers the participant to become more self-directed, and it develops fearlessness. It significantly reduces dependence in learners. Athletes and learners who are given more credit for the effort and taught to be self-directed via a shift in power from "I" to "you" benefit in several ways.

First, there is a benefit from having greater influence over the performance itself. When people are given credit for the work they put into something, they are more willing to do the work. When they realize they are the reason the results occur, they also come to understand their influence over the process. Knowing the results were directly tied to what you did, and not the magical work of some teacher or coach who waves the wand and makes you better, means you, as the performer, will begin to take control of all of your actions that lead to the outcome.

You will focus on the process, be more engaged in how you do things, and be more motivated to direct your own learning. Why? Because you know your work influences the results. You also know you will get credit for the work you did. You take the "reigns."

> **If you want to empower someone, use the word "you." "That was all you" or "You should be so proud of yourself" goes a long way in building intrinsic motivation and self-confidence.**

Allowing someone to bask in their moments of glory bestows on them a higher sense of pride. Pride, when effectively used, is a powerful motivator for transferring power to someone and creating self-reliant and self-directed performers. Telling someone they should be proud of themselves is very effective in tapping that vein of pride within them. Just as we tell someone "I believe in you" and light a fire deep within them that burns long after the game, when we transfer the power of pride to them, we help fuel that fire to burn brighter than any sun.

A person who both knows she is believed in by an influential leader and who feels a strong sense of pride is a real force of nature in performance-based situations. Whether on the field, in the classroom, or in the workplace, that person is operating from an authentic place of personal influence and motivation. Having pride means wanting to strive for mastery of techniques, wanting to seek personal excellence every time, and celebrating the effort it takes to do things "right." It means putting process over results, right over done, and performance over product. The result is still success, but the way they get there translates to success with excellence. A person with deep pride in his or her work does not cut corners, feel a need to cheat, or sweat the setbacks. They simply feel pride about all-out effort, a job well done, and being (and doing) their very best.

When we shift from "I" to "you," we also assist our charges with developing self-reliance. Do you want to joystick your athletes and students? Sure, you will get the desired results if you tell them how to do everything and take all the credit, but what happens when you are not there to control the joystick? Isn't it all about teaching them to find the answers on their own, be courageous in taking risks, and problem-solve so they can succeed on their own? We need to help them become self-reliant so they continue to strive for excellence way beyond the game.

I saw this with my son's potty training. I also saw it years later with my kindergartners learning to read, my athletes learning to play soccer, and those coaches I lead who wanted to put the very best reflection of who they were on the soccer field. Who was I to steal their moment of glory by jumping into the picture and saying, "Look at me. I did this. I am so proud of what I made you into today"?

Yet, this is what we see on the playing fields. Our kids do all the work, and we take all the credit. We guided them, but our job was to observe them solving the problems and taking the path, only to be a beacon when they needed a little light and a map when they lost the path. They should have immense pride in the work they do and be self-reliant enough to not need to look to us for the answers. "A coach," as Mark Bennett of PDS Coaching says, "should become redundant."

If you strive to do this, they will continue to succeed long after you work with them. Do you want to spend your life following all of your former students and athletes around, making sure they continue to do things exactly as you taught them, and then take all the credit? Or do you want them to go on and conquer the world on their own? They'll come back and thank you if you are willing to tell them how proud "they" should be early on and develop that self-reliance. They will never come back to say thank you for making them dependent, indecisive, and unmotivated to accomplish anything because they never developed initiative and self-reliance.

Shifting the power by using "you" also has a natural reward effect on people. They stop seeking external rewards for the work they've done, and they stop the "praise junkie" carousel we see so often in sports and other performance-based situations. People who are always looking outside themselves for that reward for a job well done tend to report an emptiness when they achieve their ultimate goals.

Super Bowl winners report feeling depressed because they thought there "would be more" when they won it. They expected some external reward and the internal feeling of success wasn't enough. Praise is praise whether it is given for going potty all by yourself or for winning a Super

Bowl. It is the same feeling, and that is so deflating to someone who felt like the praise would be amplified or different. Praise is praise. It should not be the reason you win it all.

People who spend their lives performing for others tend to burn out as well. There is no inherent feeling of accomplishment, no inner drive to excel. Only the reward of people being proud of them, and like any addiction, people will need it more and more until it is no longer enough, and then they decide to leave the carousel for good.

What if your reward was internal? Wouldn't that mean you would have a constant source of satisfaction? You would not need to hear it from others, and you would not be addicted to what others said and thought. Your addiction would be shifted to a "drive." Not for success, but for the inherent nature of the work itself.

That is the ultimate reward to a performer who does well, to feel an inner sense of reward that does not need any outside influence. That is a lifelong learner and seeker of personal excellence—a relentless and passionate worker who values the process as much as the product and who works just as hard when no one is looking as when all eyes are on him. All this comes by saying, "You should be proud of yourself," by shifting that power to the performer.

There are a few ways you can shift the power to your performers, no matter the setting, and you can do it tomorrow. Set this book down and try these immediately:

1. **Change "I" to "you" when you praise.** It is obvious, given that was the nature of the chapter, but not as easy as you might think. In settings that put you in charge, set high expectations for the outcomes of your charges, and place *you* at the center of all learning and performance standards. It is difficult not to get caught up in "I." This is your show; you are the leader, so "I" is a very natural place to go with your words. Praise with "you."

Say, "*You* should be proud of yourself," and let them understand the role they play in all of this.

2. **Stay out of the picture.** If you want to give them full power over the process, you have to give them full credit. Don't take away their credit by claiming it as your own or by, as I have seen in the past, jumping in the team picture so everyone knows your face too. Let them have their moment to shine while you hide off-camera. Point the finger at them when someone wants to give you credit. This will pay off in continued success and excellent behaviors if they get credit for the job well done. If you always jump in the picture when they win big games, they'll stop wanting to perform for you.

3. **Ask them what they want.** It seems crazy to ask athletes what they want from their sporting experience, doesn't it? I jest, but we sometimes forget to include them in the equation. If we want them to have the power, we need to transfer the power. Instead of "I want you to do this," what if we asked, "What would you do in this situation?" Now, we are creating independent-thinking problem-solvers who know they are respected by their leaders. When the time arises when we are not there to help, they will function on their own.

4. **Let them have some power.** Power is influence. Influence is a powerful ingredient for creating ownership of an experience. To help our charges with developing self-efficacy, self-reliance, a sense of pride, and accountability for their actions and outcomes, we need to allow them to have power or influence over the process. Not simply in words, by changing "I" to "you," but also by allowing them to influence everything. Start with allowing them to run halftime talks or meetings, deciding what to work on in training, or being a part of the goals and val-

ues development. It is their experience, and if they feel greater influence over it, they will step up to the challenge.

Steve Kerr, in 2018, provided us with an amazing example of what this looks like when he let his players run the timeouts during a game. Some critics berated him and said it wasn't coaching. I would argue it was the epitome of coaching. He made himself irrelevant. He coached them so well, they could coach themselves! He respected their past experiences, recognized they were the ones having to play on the court and may have a unique perspective, and gave them power over the process. We should all seek to find moments to allow our charges more influence over their learning and performance.

Chapter 7

WILL

Using "will" taps into basic human motivation.

The following is an excerpt taken from John F. Kennedy's address at Rice University on Nation's Space Effort on September 12, 1962:

> *So it is not surprising that some would have us stay where we are a little longer to rest, to wait. But this city of Houston, this State of Texas, this country of the United States was not built by those who waited and rested and wished to look behind them. This country was conquered by those who moved forward—and so will space."*

William Bradford, speaking in 1630 at the founding of the Plymouth Bay Colony, said: ". . . all great and honorable actions are accompanied with great difficulties, and both must be enterprised and overcome with answerable courage."

If this capsule history of our progress teaches us anything, it is that man, in his quest for knowledge and progress, is determined and cannot be deterred. The exploration of space will go ahead, whether we join in it or not, and it is one of the great adventures of all time. No nation that expects to be the leader of other nations can stay behind in the race for space.

Those who came before us made certain that this country rode the first waves of the industrial revolutions, the first waves of modern invention, and the first wave of nuclear power, and this generation does not intend to flounder in the backwash of the coming age of space. We mean to be a part of it; we mean to lead it. For the eyes of the world now look into space, to the moon, and to the planets beyond, and we have vowed that we shall not see it governed by a hostile flag of conquest, but by a banner of freedom and peace. We have vowed that we shall not see space filled with weapons of mass destruction but with instruments of knowledge and understanding.

Yet the vows of this nation can only be fulfilled if we in this nation are first, and, therefore, we intend to be first. In short, our leadership in science and in industry, our hopes for peace and security, [and] our obligations to ourselves as well as others, all require us to make this effort, to solve these mysteries, to solve them for the good of all men, and to become the world's leading space-faring nation.

We set sail on this new sea because there is new knowledge to be gained, and new rights to be won, and they must be won and used for the progress of all people. For, space science, like nuclear science and all technology, has no conscience of its own. Whether it will become a force for good or ill depends on man, and only if the United States occupies a position of pre-eminence can we help decide whether this new ocean will be a sea of peace or a new terrifying theater of war. I do not say that we should or will go unprotected against the hostile misuse of space any more than we go unprotected against the hostile use of land or sea, but I do say that space can be explored and mastered without feeding the fires of war, without repeating the mistakes that man has made in extending his writ around this globe of ours.

There is no strife, no prejudice, no national conflict in outer space as yet. Its hazards are hostile to us all. Its conquest deserves the best of all mankind, and its opportunity for peaceful cooperation may never come again. But why, some say, the moon? Why choose this as our goal? And they may well ask why climb the highest mountain? Why, thirty-five years ago, fly the Atlantic? Why does Rice play Texas?

We choose to go to the moon. We choose to go to the moon in this decade and do the other things, not because they are easy, but because they are hard, because that goal will serve to organize and measure the best of our energies and skills, because that challenge is one that we are willing to accept, one we are unwilling to postpone, and one which we intend to win, and the others, too.

It is for these reasons that I regard the decision last year to shift our efforts in space from low to high gear as among the most important decisions that will be made during my incumbency in the office of the Presidency.

In the last twenty-four hours, we have seen facilities now being created for the greatest and most complex exploration in man's history. We have felt the ground shake and the air shattered by the testing of a Saturn C-1 booster rocket, many times as powerful as the Atlas, which launched John Glenn, generating power equivalent to 10,000 automobiles with their accelerators on the floor. We have seen the site where the F-1 rocket engines, each one as powerful as all eight engines of the Saturn combined, will be clustered together to make the advanced Saturn missile, assembled in a new building to be built at Cape Canaveral as tall as a forty-eight-story structure, as wide as a city block, and as long as two lengths of this field.

Within these last nineteen months at least forty-five satellites have circled the earth. Some forty of them were 'made in the United States of America,' and they were far more sophisticated and supplied far more knowledge to the people of the world than those of the Soviet Union.

The Mariner spacecraft now on its way to Venus is the most intricate instrument in the history of space science. The accuracy of that shot is comparable to firing a missile from Cape Canaveral and dropping it in this stadium between the forty-yard lines.

Transit satellites are helping our ships at sea to steer a safer course. Tiros satellites have given us unprecedented warnings of hurricanes and storms and will do the same for forest fires and icebergs.

We have had our failures, but so have others, even if they do not admit them. And they may be less public.

To be sure, we are behind and will be behind for some time in manned flight. But we do not intend to stay behind, and in this decade, we shall make up and move ahead.

The growth of our science and education will be enriched by new knowledge of our universe and environment, by new techniques of learning and mapping and observation, and by new tools and computers for industry, medicine, the home as well as school. Tech-nical institutions, such as Rice, will reap the harvest of these gains.

And finally, the space effort itself, while still in its infancy, has already created a great number of new companies, and tens of thousands of new jobs. Space and related industries are generating new demands in investment and skilled personnel, and this city and this State, and this region, will share greatly in this growth. What was once the furthest outpost on the old frontier of the West will be the furthest outpost on the new frontier of science and space. Houston, your City of Houston, with its Manned Spacecraft Center, will become the heart of a large scientific and engineering community. During the next five years, the National Aeronautics and Space Administration expects to double the number of scientists and engineers in this area, to increase its outlays for salaries and expenses to $60 million a year, to invest some $200 million in plant and laboratory facilities, and to direct or con-tract for new space efforts over $1 billion from this Center in this City.

To be sure, all this costs us all a good deal of money. This year's space budget is three times what it was in January 1961, and it is greater than the space budget of the previous eight years combined. That budget now stands at $5,400 million a year—a staggering sum, though somewhat less than we pay for cigarettes and cigars every year. Space expenditures *will soon rise some more, from forty cents per person per week to more than fifty cents a week for every man, woman, and child in the United States, for we have given this program a high national priority— even though I realize that this is in some measure an act of faith and vision, for we do not now know what benefits await us.*

But if I were to say, my fellow citizens, that we shall send to the moon, 240,000 miles away from the control station in Houston, a giant rocket more than 300 feet tall, the length of this football field, made of new metal alloys, some of which have not yet been invented, capable of standing heat and stresses several times more than have ever been experienced, fitted together with a precision better than the finest watch, carrying all the equipment needed for propulsion, guidance, control, communications, food, and sur-vival, on an untried mission, to an unknown celestial body, and then return it safely to earth, re-entering the atmosphere at speeds of over 25,000 miles per hour, causing heat about half that of the temperature of the sun—almost as hot as it is here today—and do all this, and do it right, and do it first before this decade is out—then we must be bold.

I'm the one who is doing all the work, so we just want you to stay cool for a minute. [laughter]

However, I think we're going to do it, and I think that we must pay what needs to be paid. I don't think we ought to waste any money, but I think we ought to do the job. And this will be done in the decade of the sixties. It may be done while some of you are still here at school, at this college and university. It will be done during the term of office of some of the people who sit here on this platform. But it will be done. And it will be done before the end of this decade.

I am delighted that this university is playing a part in putting a man on the moon as part of a great national effort of the United States of America."

Many years ago the great British explorer George Mallory, who was to die on Mount Everest, was asked why did he want to climb it. He said, 'Because it is there.'

Well, space is there, and we're going to climb it, and the moon and the planets are there, and new hopes for knowledge and peace are there. And, therefore, as we set sail, we ask God's blessing on the most hazardous and dangerous and greatest adventure on which man has ever embarked.[3]

Will Increases Motivation

How do you get an entire country, or most likely an entire planet, to set their sights on doing the impossible?

You don't ask them. You don't share a wish or dream. No, you firmly state the outcome as if it were already a known and accomplishable task, that they "will" do it.

When John F. Kennedy delivered his now famous speech to Rice University, wherein he outlined how humankind would set foot on the moon, he put it all in perspective. He encapsulated the 50,000-year existence of humanity into a fifty-year period to show how rapidly technology and society were advancing. He created a perspective about how amazing we could be when we were determined and motivated to do something. To survive, to build cities, to find cures for diseases, to learn to fly, and to touch the stars.

He made an entire country believe they had the will to do something that was only but a dream because he first showed them all we had accomplished to date in such an incredible manner, and then, he didn't ask them to go to the moon. He told them "we will" put a man on the moon before some of them even left the school where he was speaking.

That is the unmistakable influence of the word *will* on human motivation. It triggers a psychological reaction so that multiple countries, and then an entire planet, are galvanized to conquer a vast, unrelenting, unforgiving, unknown place such as space—and to do so in a time frame that, today, seems almost miraculous. We put men on the moon, then built a space station shared by the world because we were motivated to do that. Not because we wished we could or because we had the dream . . . but because we were driven to take action by one word: *will*.

> **If a single person can use the word "will" to convince 300 million others they can do something no human has ever done on a rock floating in space some 239,000 miles from Earth, imagine what that word could do for you?**

He could have said "I hope we can" or "my wish is" or "if we could put a man on the moon . . ." But he didn't. John F. Kennedy was a master of human language and desire. He knew that by adding one word to his speech and saying it nearly thirty times in various forms throughout, he would make it resonate in the minds and hearts of everyone who heard the speech. That resonating word would be the catalyst for immense human action. We were no longer dreaming of putting people in space; we were doing it. We were no longer asking, "What if we . . ."; rather, an entire planet stated, "We *will.*"

Will is a tremendously powerful word in performance-based scenarios. It motivates people to action and gives them a clear understanding that it can (and will!) be done if they choose to do it.

It is why phrases, like "the will to compete," "the will to survive," "thy will be done," and "the will of a nation," are used so liberally in our language. Writers, thinkers, researchers, orators, and teachers know that using those phrases evokes a visceral response in the human psyche and prompts immediate and convicted action from people. Can anything deter someone who has "the will to survive?" Can anyone stop the juggernaut of "the will of a nation?"

No. Space did not stop us from accomplishing what John F. Kennedy told us we "would" do.

Will is a powerful motivator because of its very definition. It expresses future tense, inevitable events, facts about ability or capacity, or expectations about something in the future. Those definitions attach not to a vague hope or wish but to actual events that "will" occur. It is a word that indicates, by its definition, that what we are stating is inevitable. It *will* happen!

Not only *will* what we state happen, but the word is a motivator because it gives those who use it a modicum of self-efficacy. It expresses that we are fully capable and possess the skills to accomplish what we are stating. *Will* also means a desire. As we know in performances, desire is a strong emotion that can be harnessed for success. I can think of nothing more powerful than announcing that you are definitely—without a doubt—filled with total desire and fully capable and, therefore, going to do something. It is "written in the stars" because the word *will* indicates you cannot stop it; it is inevitable.

Imagine the people you lead living in an *if* world. They are not quite sure of their abilities, and they do not have a clear vision of what it would look like if they were able to accomplish what you are teaching. There is low motivation in someone who is uncertain, unclear, and unconfident, especially if what they are pursuing has never been done before. This is what John F. Kennedy was facing. Mankind had never put a human on the moon. It was 240,000 miles from home; we had no clue what the atmosphere was like, whether our ships could even get there, and what lurking dangers we had not even accounted for could be waiting for us. We were uncertain, unclear, unconfident, and completely unprepared mentally for such an endeavor.

Now imagine increasing the motivation of those you lead by changing their uncertain and unclear visions into ones of total certainty and belief by not asking them if or pondering the possibilities, but by telling them they *will* do it. Not because you told them to, but because they have ability beyond measure. You show them all they have and what others have done until now; you show them all they are capable of, and then you tell them that is why they *will* succeed. That is absolute, beautiful motivation.

That is what John F. Kennedy did! He tapped into basic human motivation with one word. He set the stage by showing us how amazing we were and how much we could accomplish if we threw ourselves into something by reminding us how capable we had always been as a species. Then, he told us we "*will* put a man on the moon." And we did.

This is what we can do with our teams if we can change the words they use with each other and with themselves and the words we use as we lead them. The formula is simple for developing the basic motivation reaction in people: show them what they and others have done, remind them how capable they are, and tell them it is inevitable—that they will succeed.

The Pieces of the Success Equation

The first piece of this success equation is best highlighted by "barrier breakers." They are the pioneers who do the one thing no one else thinks is possible, thus leading the way for others to do the same—and more.

Roger Bannister is one of the most well-known "barrier breakers" in the world. Before he came along, no one had ever run a mile in less than four minutes. Everyone said it was impossible. It could not be done by a human; we did not have the capacity to do it.

Then Bannister did it. To the astonishment of the world, he did what no human had ever done! How many people have run a sub-four-minute mile since him? He showed us the way and now serves as a beacon to anyone who dreams the impossible.

The second piece of the equation is to link that inevitable success to the individual capabilities of those you lead. It is one thing to see the successes of others and wish we could follow suit, but it's a wholly different experience to realize we, too, can achieve that goal (and others).

We need to be realistic with our charges and not tell them they can accomplish what they are truly incapable of doing. Having said that, we still need to evoke futurism in our charges by getting them to evaluate and agree with what they *are* capable of and how their capabilities are what will lead to success. This develops that sense of belief. It is not a false belief because it is scaffolded with their skills and abilities. It is a realistic belief in what they can truly accomplish.

The Power of *Will* in Visualization

Finally, don't let your athletes stay in the foggy realm of "if." Many a dream has been lost in the dense fog of uncertainty. Our charges will be uncertain, even after we show what can be done and need to be reminded about what they are capable of. It is our job to lift the fog and move them from that unclear realm of "if" to the lucidity of "will."

Employing the word *will* lifts the fog and reveals the shining sun of clarity. They can actually "see" what it is they are capable of accomplishing. *Will* is a great word to be used in visualization techniques—where you are walking athletes through exercises in their minds that give pictures of their performance. You are accounting for all contingencies, making it clear and with real vision, evoking emotional buy-in, tapping their senses, and creating a close-match mental experience of the event. In those visualization moments, you are showing them what they *will* do . . . not only showing their minds what can be done but actually getting their minds and bodies to *do* it.

Visualization causes muscle innervation. When people are doing visualization techniques, the muscles that would be recruited in the physical activity are being stimulated by the brain. What the mind sees, the body does. There is no separation between the two. They are always connected and communicating, and that is why visualization is a successful technique for preparing people to perform at their highest levels.

Of course, visualization is difficult, and there is room for more research to be done before it is honed to perfection. There are many factors involved that will either lead to success or failure with the technique, and it is difficult to employ across all performance-based scenarios.

One way it has been accomplished is through simulators. Simulators allow for leaders to perform visualization with physical activity but in an environment where it is safe to fail. Simulation is used by airlines, for instance, to help pilots train through any given scenario that may arise in flight and learn to analyze, assess, and react in ways that save lives. The simulator allows for physical accomplishment just as if the pilots were in the cockpits, but the greatest work is being done inside the brain. Pilots are learning to problem-solve, analyze, remain calm, and train the brain for success.

For most of us leaders, simulators do not make much sense and are not affordable. Visualization can also be difficult due to age considerations, environments, and a lack of training. But there is one visualization facet that can be employed tomorrow without the need for machines, training, or extensive research. Simply show athletes what has been done, remind them of what they can do, and tell them they *will* do it. Here is how you can use *will* tomorrow to motivate your teams:

1. Help them change peril words like try, maybe, can't, or if to will. The human brain wants to revert to its lizard brain and protect us at all costs. This is not simply about physical threats. It happens during mental and emotional threats too. When faced with the possibility of mental or emotional harm, the brain will tread lightly. It will be cautious, and this is illuminated by the use of cautious words. Performers who are uncertain, exercising caution, or lacking confidence will use words that allow the brain an excuse for either not trying at all or justifying any future failure.

For instance, saying "try" means a person can either choose at the last minute not to do something—because it was a tenuous commitment in the first place—or if they fail, allows them to give the excuse, "Well, I tried, but couldn't do it." That is much safer for the psyche, but it does not motivate people to achieve things outside of their comfort zones. Our role is to help people expand their comfort zones to accomplish things they never thought they could do so they can continue to grow and improve. Our role is to observe others achieving personal excellence, and excellence is all about doing the very best with what you have at the moment. This means stretching to be better than you were yesterday. That is excellence.

To better serve in our role, we need to shift their words, and ours, from those peril words that let them stay comfortable and cautious. By simply switching out *try, maybe, can't,* or *if* with the word *will,* we are shifting their motivation to one of inevitability. It is no longer *whether* they can do something, but *that* they can, should expect to, and *will* do it. Plain and simple, it says: "You got this."

1. Employ the motivation equation discussed above. The teams we lead look to us for guidance and strength. They need us to keep the light shining when the fog of uncertainty is settling on them. The easiest way to motivate and give clarity to our charges is to show them what has been done, remind them of what they can do, and tell them they *will* do it.

In these situations, *will* is not a demand. It has to be an inevitability statement. You are not a dictator telling people they have to do something "or else." You are a mentor, confidant, and guide who is cheering them on and showing them a path. Instead of holding the proverbial torch to their rear ends and forcing them, you pass them the torch and tell them you believe in them. This is done by the equation and finishing with that all-important inevitability of the word *will*.

My son loves technology and wants to be a coder. He was taking a class in school that gave him access to some app-building software, but he told me he couldn't create apps yet because he was too young and didn't know enough. We researched other coders, their ages, and the stories of those who taught themselves how to code. Of course, Silicon Valley is rife with these stories. You can throw a rock in Campbell, California, and hit a successful someone who was "too young and didn't know enough yet."

I told him, "If they can do it, it can be done. You have a brain that loves learning; you love technology, and when you visited Qualcomm, they told you that you had a coder's mind. So if it can be done and you have what it takes, why not you? Want to bet you will build one?"

I forgot all about the conversation until the end-of-year project tours, when his technology teacher showed me his new app. He had built an app that translates spoken Spanish into typed and spoken English and vice versa—all on his own!

His teacher was so impressed, she told him he will have his own app in the App Store by the end of high school. I was blown away. I was also out $50 for a video game because of that bet.

Use simple visualization with affirmations and performance statements. If you have a few minutes to spare, you have more than enough time to help your team mentally prepare for success. Take those few moments to circle them up and guide them through some visualization. It does not need to be in-depth or scientifically relevant; it just needs to tap into their motivation centers and provide some neural priming for the performance.

The circle is key. It signifies comfort. It is oneness, safety, and equality among all. It also means people can see everyone's eyes, and this creates a mental and emotional connection that allows for greater brain activation. As people see the emotions in others' eyes, they achieve deeper brain activity.

Once in the circle, walk them through all they have done to get to this moment. The hard work, the training, the skills they have acquired, and the accomplishments to date. Show them what has been done and remind them of what they can do through affirmations. Be strong, confident, and loving in your language. You are speaking directly to their neurons now. You are holding a match to their neurons to light the fire, so to speak.

Finally, keep the fire burning in those darned neurons with a few *will* statements. Talk them quickly through the performance. Describe the emotions, smells, tastes, and sights to take their brains to the actual event. The neurons are firing rapidly now. The muscles are priming, and the brain is lit up with activity as you walk them through the moments and tell them what *will* happen. That is the big key: telling them what they will do, how they will act, and what they will accomplish today. Your language should be firm, loving, powerful, and inevitable. They *will*.

You just Bravehearted the heck out of your charges without needing to wear a kilt, don blue face paint, and deliver the speech of your lifetime. I've done both in my career. I once delivered a speech of a lifetime, totally unscripted and in the moment, that my athletes still talk about nearly eight years later, but that was once. Many times over, I have used this "will visualization" technique with the same kind of success, and those athletes also still talk about it. Take the easy route and do this technique to tap into the motivation centers of your athletes.

Will Moves People Beyond Failure

When performers fail, you must move them forward with *will*. In moments of failure, the brain reacts with all kinds of neural activity. It is looking for safety, a way to protect us. It is assessing damage, a place for blame, and how to demotivate us from ever doing that again (because it mentally hurt). This is when we all need to be motivated the most.

Instead of yelling at your athletes or team—or worse, punishing them—try motivating them for the next time. Pick them up with some positive reinforcement and encouragement to do it again by telling them it is okay, that you are there to help them get where they want to go, and they will get there. They *will*.

This is all it takes. They know failure is part of the process, and it's expected along every journey, so we don't react violently to it, but rather, take it in stride. They know they are supported and loved when we tell them we will help them. People accomplish extraordinary things when they know someone is holding the rope. Finally, they stop worrying about what happened and start focusing on what they will do.

This is especially effective with younger people. Getting them to move past the failure and focus on how they *will* get it is key. Giving them a clear vision of the future with support to help them get there is a very intense motivator. Try it. You *will* see amazing results!

Chapter 8

WHAT IF

Use "what if" as a lighthouse beacon to help others see what it is they want to accomplish, who they can be, and what their next choice should be.

I was frustrated, and my wife knew it. I felt like I was spinning my wheels and wasting my life. Like a car stuck in the mud, I was going nowhere fast and making a huge mess of everything.

She had been quietly listening to my rant for going on twenty minutes. I was complaining about the lack of respect I perceived for what I did as a "hobby." I was yelling about the ultimatum my employer had delivered to me and the unfairness of the whole thing. I was trapped in a job I knew I did not want to be doing. I was simply fed up with it all.

I had been in the fundraising realm for nearly seven years at the time and felt thoroughly unfulfilled. It is a great job with great benefits and fantastic personal rewards. It pays very well. There is a level of prestige that comes with it (I was working for one of the largest and most successful charities in America, and we were certainly changing lives). I could travel a lot and meet interesting people. There was nothing wrong with the job—except it wasn't me. I felt like a caged lion.

Two Words Made Me Quit My Job

I knew my love: coaching. Educating. My passion was for sports and using them as a vehicle for transforming lives. The sports world was also a hobby. It didn't pay well. It was not well-respected, and it also caused a stir at work.

I had recently been quoted in a local newspaper that was doing a story on the high school team I coached. I had been coaching for two decades, always after work and always as a side job. I had recently taken a high school coaching job and loved it, but it brought a little press with it. At least in the local paper. It was a small paper and an even smaller quote, but it somehow crossed the desk of one of the executives at the charity.

I worked remotely out of Cincinnati, and my boss, the vice president, was in Philadelphia. His boss was in DC. The article was printed in an Oxford, Ohio, paper, yet somehow, she saw it. It was a great article and painted me in a positive light. I thought it was good public relations.

She didn't see it that way. She felt it conflicted with my role at the organization. She believed it was a distraction from my day job and also detracted from the prestige of my role as a senior development officer. Who knew being a soccer coach was such a bad thing?

My boss was given an ultimatum by his boss to deliver to me. *Stop coaching soccer or I could be out of work.* I knew of several other employees of this organization who were Sunday School teachers too. I had a colleague who worked at a coffee shop on the weekends for the free coffee and to help cover her kids' college tuition. They weren't given any ultimatum. I was.

I was angry. I love coaching. Why should I give it up? I was skilled at it, and it brought good press. Why would it detract from my role with the nonprofit? I didn't understand.

So there I was, laying all of my anger out in front of my wife. "I get no respect. I work my tail off. I have a right to coach on the side if I want. What about the employees who volunteer to coach their kids? Should they quit too? This is what I love, and I can't make a living at it. In fact, I am now being told I have to quit doing it for a job I don't even like."

At that moment, my wife stopped my rant. She always knew I had been miserable, but suddenly, I was admitting it. I openly named my unfulfilment. She had known I was dying a small death inside and felt like I was not doing what I was put on this earth to do . . . now she had proof.

The first thing you need to know about my wife is that she is my biggest fan and greatest supporter. Her initial response was a defiant and confident statement: *I would not quit coaching.* She knew that was my "one thing," and she would not let me abandon it. The short version of the story has always been that she helped me realize I needed to chase my Everest by telling me to quit my day job, but I took more convincing than that.

The longer version is as follows: She helped me craft a perfect clarification of purpose in my own head and heart by helping me with perspective. Through her, I could see things differently with a few words.

"Oh, honey. I see you. I see that look every morning when you leave the house. Like you are losing a piece of your soul because you can't do what you love full time. I see the look you have when you head to soccer. Pure joy. I see how you are on that field—like you were born to do that."

She paused and let her words sink in a moment.

"What if money were not an issue? What if you could do what you wanted and not worry about feeding the kids or putting a roof over everyone's head? What would you do if you could do what you were meant to do?"

"I would coach full-time!" There was no hesitation in my answer. It was the surest I had been of something in a long time (since the day I met her and told my buddy I was going to marry her).

"Well . . ." was her only response.

What If Clarifies Purpose

What if was all it took to clarify my purpose in life. Those two words took me from dreaming to reality and gave me the strength, courage, and resolve to change course and do what I love. It's not that a career in development is a bad thing. It paid well, and the organization treated us well. It was safe. I worked for a great charity that was changing the world. It just wasn't what I *loved*.

My wife knew this much, and she also knew I was stuck in a rut. I was not clear on my purpose. Her words helped me gain clarity about what I wanted out of life and where I wanted to be. Simply put, they gave me *resolve* because they gave me a laser focus on what I should be doing.

That evening, I enrolled in a Master's of Education program, reached out to my club about being more full-time as a coach, and wrote up a resignation letter. By Monday morning, I had resigned from the rat race and the "working class" and was running headlong into the life I live now.

This isn't some fairy tale with the ride-off-into-the-sunset ending. This new life path has been tough. My wife worked bartending jobs, worked in daycare, and was even a nanny just to help make ends meet while I finished up my second M.S. degree, one that would help me be a better coach and professional in my realm.

We've borrowed money from both sets of parents; we've had to hold our breaths when rent checks were sent in, and we've raided the change jar on many occasions to put gas in the car. All the while, though, we have enjoyed every single moment of this glorious adventure.

This adventure has paved the way for me to give a TEDx Talk, allowed me to travel throughout the United States and internationally—seeing places I would have never seen—and compelled us to move across the country to San Diego (which may have been the greatest decision we ever made). I've made amazing friends, worked with world-class organizations, and spent every day I possibly can on the beach.

All this because my wife was brave enough to ask "what if," and I was just crazy enough to answer honestly.

This is the power we give to our athletes when we are willing to help them clarify their purposes, when they are struggling to see a light at the end of the tunnel or grinding through a hard season. This is the opportunity we have to elevate their gaze beyond a single moment, such as when they've fallen down.

Youth sports is more than a difficult journey. It is a jagged, uneven, narrow mountain pass as kids cope with learning to play a sport in a foggy environment, navigate slippery social interactions, and avoid the fallen rocks of self-doubt. We lump massive amounts of pressure on them when we focus on outcomes, scholarships, and specialization. Then we expect them to cherish the journey and see a glorious future.

They can barely see past the next practice drill, let alone understand the joy of mastery, success, and life fulfillment that can come from playing youth sports.

Add to that our constant desire to create problem-solvers out of them . . . and it is too much to reconcile. They play head down, blinders on, just trying to get to the next water break. The future is uncertain because their purpose is unclear.

Imagine being able to lift the fog and help them see clearly. Words like *what if* are the lighthouse beacon that can help them see what it is they want to accomplish, who they can be, and what their next choice should be.

What if holds the power to provide clarity of purpose and also the clarity of decision-making because it gives their minds the freedom to imagine and create possible solutions and outcomes for the problems they face.

For a team, the purpose is a binding agent. You don't have to look much further than the New Zealand All Blacks to see what a team with a shared purpose can accomplish. The mission has always been the same, no matter who wore the black jersey with the silver fern: continue the legacy.

Each new team member is given a small, black book in which all of the sayings, jerseys, standards, and advice of players past reside. This book is their guide, giving them purpose. Their *what ifs* that set their minds on a mission and their eyes on a target.

Sit down with a team and ask them *what if*, and watch the purpose slowly, but powerfully, evolve from nothing. As a season continues and you remind them of that purpose, witness their growth from a group of players doing their own thing to a family of human beings focused on one common goal. *What if* translates *what they do* to *why they do it*. Imagine being courageous enough to dream of infinite possibilities, even about the impossible.

What if gave us the Miracle on Ice. *What if* gave us the Jamaican bobsled team, the curse-breaking 2016 Chicago Cubs, the Doug Flutie finish, and every other Hail Mary we've had the glory of experiencing or witnessing. What if fuels dreams and dreams relentlessly hunted by a resolute athlete or group of athletes are the moments of magic in sports.

Hitting even closer to home for those of us who coach youth sports is the power of *what if* to help children get to the other side of failure. When a child is stumped, has fallen, or is not quite able to grasp the answer, asking *what if* allows them to step away from the stressful moment, take a breath, and think about solutions. It is not just *what if,* but anything that begins with the word *what* can be the catalyst for growth in our athletes.

> ## Many great moments started with a quiet, "What if?"

The next time an athlete shows "that look," which says "I'm stuck" or "I need help," instead of jumping in with the answer, try asking *what if.*

"What if a teammate were open and could relieve the defensive pressure?"

"I would pass it to them and then find a better spot to get open and get the ball back, coach."

"Look around. Anyone open?"

The lightbulb might go off.

"What could you do here that could get you out of this . . ."

"What would it look like if . . ."

"What is another way to . . ."

These questions are open-ended. Like essay questions on a test, there are many right answers and many possible answers for the kids to work through. It opens a door to a world of opportunity when they may have only seen true or false as possible solutions. It gives them the chance to explain their reasoning and work through the problem.

The beauty of essay questions for those of us with growth mindsets is that we may not be sure of the answer, but we know if we work through the problem presented to us with enough data, support, proof, and options, we might at least get partial credit. Partial credit is much better than a zero.

Athletes need to see partial credit as much as they need to solve. Partial credit allows them to get rewarded for the effort and still work toward more viable solutions. It prevents the fatality most experience by quitting at the first obstacle. It allows them to be analytical, fearless, and honest.

I've always encouraged my players to have the courage to fail, the honesty to admit it, and the fortitude to fix it. Athletes with this belief ask, "What if I try this?" This is the summary of *what if.*

It may not work every time, but they know I want them to work through it and be honest about what did work and what didn't, then ask *what if* again, and work through it again. I coach them to have the fortitude to fix it.

Creating clarity of purpose and resilience in athletes is much easier than we know if we are willing to ask more questions, give fewer answers, and be merciful in moments of failure.

To create clarity of purpose, sit your team down and give them ownership of the team's mission, vision, and goals. Ask them the questions, and they will provide the answers. Because they've created those answers and the team culture, there is a sense of purpose and ownership. They hold themselves and each other accountable. Sometimes, they even hold the coach accountable if the empowerment is strong enough inside them.

Another way to help athletes is to add *what if* to the front of their requests. Athletes will ask coaches for permission throughout their careers. Most coaches either say yes or no, but this is like a true and false question on a test. They are fifty/fifty for failing. By adding *what if,* you are asking them to present you with essays. To provide facts or proof to support their requests. You are getting them to think more deeply. They will discover their request was not worth it, or they will recognize the magic in that request and feel empowered because they concluded on their own.

You can also pose more questions in training in a more Socratic way. Instead of freezing athletes, showing a picture, and then giving the solution, try asking them questions. Freeze them and ask, "What do you see?" Ask them *what if* [blank] happened. Get them thinking with "what could or should you do" questions. Encourage them to take a chance by saying, "Okay, what if we tried this? Let's try it and see."

What a powerful way to coach athletes! They have clarity of purpose and gain the resolve to see it through—and build the courage to ask questions that will yield new answers. This is the kind of journey that not only builds healthy, resilient, and courageous athletes. It builds healthy, resilient, and courageous people.

What if we created more people like that?

Chapter 9

WE

———◆———

People who hear "we language" from their leaders have greater trust in them, higher respect for them, and more resilient responses to setbacks.

They had a winning streak of 111 games. They had a chance to win a third straight National Championship. They had a chance at immortality in sport, and sadly, when those rare and amazing streaks ended, they seemed marred by the loss. The focus became the loss.

We Just Weren't Ready

As we are prone to do, we search for a reason for such epic falls. We look for meaning to make us feel better about witnessing something so great come to an end. If we lose after only a three-game win streak, no one bats an eye. No one points the cold finger of blame. When someone loses after 111 games, people want answers. Somehow, the stakes are higher when 111 games and immortality are on the line.

So it goes. UConn women's basketball carried 111 straight games and held two straight national championship tiles going into the Final Four, and they lost. As Geno Auriemma stood outside his team's locker room addressing the press, he was pressed for answers. Who cares that they won 111 straight—the most and by absolute dominance! People needed to know what went *wrong* in this one game.

Here is why I love coaches like Geno and what they do for the athlete's mind: He is a coach that does not always say the right things, but his intentions are always to build people up and elevate performance. His words held power. His answer to the question was nothing short of perfect.

"Maybe we're just not ready for this . . . maybe all our young kids needed to experience this so we can come back and be ready for this."

With a simple and honest sentence, Geno Auriemma put perspective on this one loss. He accepted responsibility for his role in the loss. He also shifted the locus of control for his players.

Coach Geno could have pointed to mistakes his players made. He could have blamed the refs for the loss. Maybe the playing conditions were poor for his team. Coaches have certainly pointed those fingers in days past. Or he could have even said the other team was just better. We would have accepted those excuses. We would have run with them and analyzed them until we were bored with it or a new season began.

Instead, he used a word of great power to reframe the loss and move on from it. *We.* He said, "We're just not ready for this," meaning they (the team and coaches) have full control over their performance at all times.

The loss is not because of some external factor that cannot be controlled by the players. Something that excuses their actions, protects their fragile egos, and deflects fault. Saying it was an external factor would be so much easier to swallow and would allow them to cling to the purity of that 111-game win streak. But that would not have been a good long-game strategy. The coach shouldered it all. He allowed the loss to become something of total control. He eclipsed the beauty of the streak for the magic of the process. By saying, "We're just not ready," he ensured the power stayed with the players. They could work. They could adjust. They could go home, throw themselves into getting better, and be ready for next time. No one can control refs, other teams, or playing conditions. We can control how we prepare.

Coach Geno also gave all leaders who were listening a powerful lesson on humility, responsibility, and our role as those obligated to guide others to their best performances. He could have said, "They weren't ready," and in the eyes of all of his adoring fans, he would have remained one of the best coaches in basketball. He had no part in the loss; his players let him down, right?

Wrong. Geno said, "We" because he believes the "strength of the pack is the wolf, and the strength of the wolf is the pack." He knows that a great culture is all-in together and, win or lose, they all play a role. His courage to use the word *we* binds them as one. Coach and players are connected.

The word also invites a level of responsibility for his role. He didn't blame his players, taking on the air of a coach who is always at the top of their game, and whereby the players just let them down in the game. No. A team not ready is not ready because the coach didn't fulfill all of their duties. It is our job to help them prepare. Just because we taught them, doesn't mean they learned it. We must make sure they've learned it, and if they didn't, it is our fault.

As John Wooden once said, "Failure is not fatal, but failure to change might be." This loss to Geno and his team was not fatal. They would adapt; they would adjust, and they would return and be ready. They would not fail to change.

For true competitors, those with a warrior essence, losing is painful, but it is not seen as a flaw in the warrior or a defining characteristic of their nature. Failure is simply an experience, one from which they can learn, grow, and recover. Elite warriors have as many scars as they do trophies because failure—and all of the development that comes with it—is part of their very essence.

Geno is a warrior of the highest order because he was willing to be down in the trenches with his Huskies and accept a role in the failure and seek to move on by focusing on what he could control. You better believe they will be ready next time with that kind of outlook.

We Changes the Locus of Control to Internal

We should all strive to have *we* language with those we lead and teach. *We* builds connection. It is a word that ties us with those around us. *We* states responsibility. It gives us a place to start for accountability and recovery. *We* also shifts the locus of control. It gives us and our athletes the power to know we are always in full control of how we perform.

People who hear *we* language from their leaders have greater trust in them, higher respect for them, and more resilient responses to setbacks. You can use this more often in several situations to shift the locus of control for your charges.

> **"We" leverages the excellence of the entire group and minimizes the vulnerability of the individual.**

In moments of success, when praise is being tossed at you as the leader, always punctuate the word *we*. If someone says, "You set a high mark this week," for instance, your response should be, "We sure did set a high mark." Or even better, use "they" to give all the credit to those who carried the bulk of the load.

In moments of failure, be quick to insert *we* in all of your language. Be sure your team knows the setback was not all on them, but that you played a role in the defeat as well. Make certain they also hear the *we* so they know this is something that can be changed.

Finally, when trying to seek buy-in from teams, be sure to talk about *we*. I noticed early in my career that I gravitated toward the teammates, the coaches, and the staff who treated an organization like a family. People who tended to talk about "they" or "you" when referring to a place where they worked or played were the ones who rarely seemed to fully connect. They were on the outside looking in or were waiting to move on to the next thing. I never fully trusted or engaged with them, but someone who used *we* language had my loyalty from the start.

Shifting the locus of control is a powerful method for developing warrior performers and for creating unity. We can do it if we simply change a word or two.

Chapter 10

YET

———◆———

"Yet" is the hopeful, nearby, and fully attainable future
we need our children to see.

In 2008, David Segal had been in talks with a Sri Lankan tea seller to buy his newly created loose-leaf teas. The seller owned a boutique store, and David wanted to be a supplier to gain a foothold in the expanding loose-leaf tea market.

The seller was not very interested, but out of respect for David, he heard his pitch. Instead of giving a flat-out no and shutting down the relationship for good, the seller told David, "Not yet." He left the door ajar for a future opportunity, and later, David turned the *not yet* into a *yes*.

A Not Yet Worth $40 Million

Nine years later, David's Teas is still going strong, but David hadn't quite learned the lesson yet. He recalls a time when a startup met him for a few breakfasts in Montreal to discuss their app. It was built to help people find spaces in which to meditate or stretch. David, not seeing the potential, gave them a flat no.

The idea was reiterated a few times until it became an app for on-the-go professionals to find small office spaces to rent by the hour. The app, called Breather, expanded to New York and in late 2016, it closed a $40 million funding round.

What David learned is the flat-out no had ended everything at that moment. He didn't get a second chance to get involved with Breather. In contrast, his Sri Lankan tea seller left room for future opportunities by saying, "Not yet," and because of it, David successfully launched and grew David's Teas.

Think about the ramifications of a flat no. How many times have conversations been ended, hopes been shut down, or opportunities been missed because we spoke with such finality?

I am not against saying no. Many times, I have held my sanity only through being able to say no . . . usually more like "not tonight" or "not now" so I leave the door open for the next time. What I am against is the complete finality of words like *can't, no, won't,* or *not.* Words that shut down a future in the mind of an athlete. Whether spoken by the athlete or by someone else, these words have a devastating impact on the performer's mindset. It is fixed. Final. No possibility. What is done is done.

Imagine the power of three letters in one word. *Yet.* It leaves hope on the table. It hints at a future possibility, and it conveys that something is attainable in a short time with some work. This is a word all athletes should be quite familiar with and should use regularly. It is a word that Carol Dweck used to spark millions of minds across the world when she gave her famous TED Talk called "The Power of Yet."

In her talk, Carol explains that a school in Chicago started giving "not yet" grades instead of failing the students. There were certain classes the students needed to pass to graduate, and if a student was told *not yet*, he or she could still have a chance to pass it.

Not yet, or *yet*, shows a belief that we are on a trajectory of learning. An ascension, so to speak, as we develop. We were not born with all the skills, and our abilities are not final; we have the opportunity to get better and accomplish tomorrow what we couldn't today.

Yet is a bridge in the mind. It spans time for us from the present moment to an attainable future. It places failures and setbacks on this timeline as part of the greater journey, as waypoints, instead of being final stops or endings. It treats mistakes as a normal part of the trip we take in learning novel things.

Consider the idea of traveling across the country by car. Let's say your trip goes from Cincinnati, Ohio, to San Diego, California. When you first hop in your car and drive a few hours into Indianapolis, only about a hundred miles, you come across a sign that reads, "Welcome to Indianapolis" and another that says, "St. Louis 100 miles."

If you saw this sign, you could panic and think, "I didn't make it to San Diego. I can't get there!" That sounds silly. Of course, you wouldn't make it to San Diego in only a few hours, and of course, you pass through Indianapolis on your way! It seems absurd to quit at that point. In this scenario, you are headed in the right direction and simply need to be patient.

Those signs are feedback that you are on course—just as we receive feedback during learning that tells us we are on course. It is part of the entire trip, and it's commonplace to look for those signs so you can gauge how far you've gone, how much you have left, and how you are doing.

What if the sign read, "Welcome to Pittsburgh"? If you knew your maps and planned the trip ahead of time, you would know you went in the wrong direction. Would you then throw your hands up and say, "I can't do this. I won't make it!" No. I hope not.

You may curse a little and flip your map over (it was upside down, duh), but you would use that sign as feedback as well. It was a mistake. It's negative feedback, but it lets you know to correct course and try again. It is also part of the trip. You can use that sign in the same way you used the Indianapolis sign. The signs are part of the journey.

The Pittsburgh sign is just like failing or making mistakes in sports. We're made aware that we messed up, but in sports, we tend to give up in those moments where we get those negative feedback signs (a.k.a, losses). When we cannot acquire a skill automatically, as easily as our avatars in video games, for example, we quit. We toss in the towel and proclaim to the world we weren't born to do this.

Yet transforms failure into potential.

Think back to David's Teas. If the tea seller had said no, he would have missed out on a great opportunity, just as David did with Breather. What if David had quit when he heard no? What if Breather had thrown in the towel when David didn't think their idea had legs? Both either kept going or corrected course, and the ability to see past the *no* moment allowed them to cash in on millions and build successful companies.

Growth Mindset

Continued learning is the power of *yet* for our athletes. The ability to set a growth mindset that says if we have not reached our city yet, we can check the road signs and keep going. When my children are riding in the car, the question they ask the most is, "Are we there yet?" They trust me to get them to their destination safely and, sometimes, in due time. As a coach, I hope my players see me in the same light. I hope when they are learning they think, "Are we there yet? If not, I know Coach Reed will get us there safely and in due time."

We give our athletes that kind of trust, resilience, and effort mindset when we teach them to believe in the power of *yet*. Instead of thinking they can't do things, meaning *ever*, we can help them shift to knowing they may not be able to do it now, but with effort, focus, and resilience, they will soon be able to do it.

Yet is the hopeful, nearby, and fully attainable future we need our children to see. Instead of seeing life as a series of unfortunate events in which they are constantly faced with failure and loss, they could see life as full of challenges that make them better, make the journey exciting, and are filled with wonder and hope. They come to cherish the challenge more than the arrival itself because life is lived, as I like to tell my kids ad nauseam, "on the side of the mountain" not in the valley of comfort.

Here are four things the power of *yet* can do for our athletes and ways we can cultivate them to help our athletes embrace the power.

1. ***Yet* creates a growth mindset.** It allows athletes to realize their skills and abilities are not fixed at birth; rather, they can learn and accomplish new things if they are willing to cherish the challenge and put in the work. Teach them to see yet as a battle cry for battling on like little warriors unwilling to stop at the first sign of resistance. This is easy to teach but takes time and repetition. When your athletes say they *can't* do something, you have to happily claim, "Yet! You mean you *can't yet?*" Teach them to tack *yet* on the end of their statements to develop that growth mindset.

2. ***Yet* builds resilience.** The worst thing we can do for our athletes is to teach them to quit. Even when the chips are fully stacked against us, we need to believe in the power of *yet* and teach our athletes to always bridge that gap between the insurmountable odds of now to the attainable success of the future. We will not

always win or learn the skills, but the battle makes us tough. Learning to lose, having given all you had, is as much a growth or development moment as winning, if not more. They learn to always press on in the face of challenges. This builds resilience for life. When our teams lost, we told them one of two things: 1) We were not ready to win this game yet, but it has prepared us for the next time. We have yet to reach our full potential. 2) We will use this game to learn for the future. We have not learned all we were supposed to yet and needed to lose to learn a bit more. The season is not over yet. (If it is, there is always next year).

3. ***Yet* focuses athletes on mastery and process instead of outcomes.** An athlete focused on outcomes will cut corners, finish as quickly as possible, or do what is only necessary to get the job done. My son is notorious for speeding through his homework so it is done and he can mark it off as such. He will sacrifice great grades for mediocre grades if it means getting things done. He is now learning the value of mastery. Mastering the learning allows him to do well on tests, embeds the skill for later use, and gives him a better sense of accomplishment. In sports, athletes who want only outcomes succumb easily to cheating or taking the easy route. Youth sports don't exist to teach kids that; they exist to teach them new skills, life lessons, and values. Learning to embrace *yet* means being willing to master new skills, seek personal excellence, and stay focused on the process. You can't look at the end if you have both eyes focused on the path. You also don't fall off the path if you have both eyes on it. Teach them to focus on the path and not the outcome.

4. ***Yet* builds a sense of trust.** An athlete who is taught *yet* is like my kids in the back of the car. They have no idea how close they

may be to their destination, but they are ever-hopeful and will trust you implicitly.

"Are we there yet?" they ask from the back seat. They know the answer is probably no. They also know I won't steer them wrong. I made a promise to deliver them, and I will keep it. They are safe in that car and will arrive because I will keep my word. They may be a little curious, sometimes impatient, but they never fail to believe we will make it.

Then they return to their videos because they are enjoying the journey. They know they will get there in due time.

It's okay to be impatient. It means you are seeking excellence, but the impatience must be tempered with a belief you are headed in the right direction and that you will get there in due time.

You can see the power of *yet*, and why one of the world's leading experts on mindset used *yet* to fill a TED Talk. It has this amazing ability to transform what we say from a failed stop to a hopeful belief in a bigger destination.

Chapter 11

NEXT

―――――◆――――――

The issue is that performers think they have to live in that moment, or, more precisely, they think that moment is what defines them.

It was a blustery, chilly fall day in southwestern Ohio. I was coaching in a youth soccer tournament (when wasn't I coaching back in the heyday?) and had a few minutes to kill between games. I had just finished up my "under-fourteen boys" game and was walking across the rain-soaked soccer complex toward my next game with my "under-ten girls" team. As I tramped along, feet sloshing in the thick, wet, cold grass, one of my colleagues caught my eye.

Andy was coaching one of his teams on a field close to where my next game would take place, so I joined him on the bench for a few minutes. This was one of my favorite aspects of coaching in a large club. I saw our teams everywhere and ran into my colleagues often. At the more heavily attended tournaments, I would write out the schedule of all the teams under my director of coaching purview and see as many snippets of games in a weekend as I could handle. (My record is nineteen games in two days.) I didn't see the entire game, but enough to do an evaluation of the team and coach to help them get better.

Andy was my co-director, so I did not need to evaluate his team, but I loved spending time on the bench with the players, watching their progress, and learning from coaches like Andy. I have to be honest. I will watch nearly any coach do his or her job simply out of curiosity, but few in my club at the time had my respect like Andy had. He was calm, intelligent, spoke genuinely and kindly to the players, and simply knew his stuff. It was always a treat to learn from him. I nearly always came away from watching him with a new tactic, phrase, or better way to approach sideline and game management. He was a real treat to watch.

This day would be no different from the norm. I asked if I could join him and the team and settled in to watch and learn. Mere minutes passed before I was gifted one of my favorite words, which I have since used more often than I can count.

One of Andy's players attempted a pass right in front of her own goal and mis-hit it. It squibbed to an opposing player who was in an advantageous position to score. Andy's player immediately put her head down and muttered something negative.

Fortunately for her, the opponent did not get a clear look at the goal, and the ball sailed wide. Andy's player was still visibly upset, but without hesitation, and instinctually, Andy called out, "Next!"

She looked at him and gave a thumbs up . . . and a small smile crept across her face. The moment of doubt, fear, and frustration passed for her. It was a brilliant coaching moment.

Of course, Andy knew me well enough to realize I would be taking notes about that moment. He turned to me and explained his word.

"My players tend to get stuck on a single moment. A failure, a mistake, a mis-hit. They let that rule the rest of their game. I don't want them to get stuck in the moment of failure. I want them to move beyond it. So I say, 'Next' to remind them to fix it on the next touch, make up for it with the next shot, improve the next time."

It was one of those rare moments when I knew instantly that I would be transformed as a coach if I chose to use that simple word.

It Isn't What Happens to You; It Is What You Do Next That Matters

We do not always know the things that make us better. We muddle through as coaches and leaders hoping for that 1 percent increase in our abilities each day so we can look back years later and see how far we have come and how many lives we've changed. But that moment was one when I knew it would make a 100 percent improvement in my coaching.

> **Next moves a person from the quicksand of self-doubt to the ocean of possibility.**

With one word, Andy moved his athletes past those sometimes lethal failure moments. Many of us mess up, then get in our own heads about our mess up, and spend the rest of the game stuck in that moment. It spirals out of control, and we mess up even more until we are in a full-blown mental meltdown. Or, at the very least, we get stuck in that moment so much so that we never try that thing again.

Next Moves Beyond Failure Moments

The goal for a coach in those moments is to get athletes beyond them. Remember John Wooden's famous quote: "Failure is not fatal, but failure to change might be." In other words, our athletes cannot see failure as the final result, ever. Failure is not permanent unless we quit at that very moment.

If I make a mistake, I fail, and then I quit trying, then my decision to not try again is what made the mistake permanent, and, of course, fatal in my mind. The specialty athletes who perform solo in front of a crowd, and on whose shoulders the game—perhaps for an entire team—rests, know this concept well. The kicker called to make the game-winning field goal, the goalie called to stop the penalty kick in the final moments, the point guard who needs to make both one-and-ones to win the game. They know if they miss, they will lose the game, but the key for those athletes is not to make a miss a fatality moment for their careers. They must step up and try again the next time. A failure followed by the commitment to change or move on is only a mere step in the process of growth. A failure followed by quitting makes everything a full stop for athletes and coaches alike.

Andy's use of the word *next* was one of the more brilliant methods I had ever seen to get players to avoid making failure fatal. To move beyond a moment and change for the next one. *Next* became a stalwart mantra for most of the teams I coached after that day. When a player messed up, we would call out "Next!" and they knew we had faith in them to get it next time; they knew it was okay to make mistakes and move forward, and they knew the game was moving too quickly to get stuck in a single moment.

No one wants to live life stuck in a moment, like a record skipping on a word or a movie repeating the same clip again and again. No one wants to end their career in that kind of failure loop. The issue is that athletes think they have to live in that moment, or, more precisely, they think that moment is what defines them.

Athletes believe this because coaches yell at them when they mess up and brand that moment into their psyche. They think this because coaches sub them out of the game and punish them for the mistake, making that moment fatal. They know this because everyone focuses myopically on that very moment, giving it permanence.

What if coaches could tell athletes, "It's okay to mess up, but what are you going to do about it?" Or what if coaches showed them that they are not judged by their mistakes but by how they react to them? How much more confident, focused, and innovative would athletes be if they had the freedom to mess up and the strength to move beyond their failure moments?

Next gives them that freedom and strength. In one word, it says, "Have the courage to fail, the honesty to admit it, and the fortitude to fix it." *Next* is the kind of word that can be quickly deployed to keep your athletes focused, disciplined, and moving forward rather than looking backward.

This kind of mentality crafted in an entire team creates fearlessness (which we will discuss in our "Love" section), focus, discipline, and confidence. When entire teams are reminding each other to get to the *next* touch, play the *next* ball, or fix it with the *next* shot, they are staying grounded, playing in the present moment, instead of being stuck in the past and allowing failure to become permanent.

Strive to use *next* in your coaching. Begin in training to introduce it to your players. If you do it in a game, they will have no idea what you mean. When it is introduced, be sure to explain the meaning behind the word—that you do not want them to focus on what went wrong, but focus on moving forward and getting better with every opportunity. You want them to learn and grow from mistakes rather than be defined by them.

Once you have introduced the word in training, toss it out there in games. When a player messes up, don't yell. Don't be demonstrative (a coach's body language screams as loudly as our words), and don't punish them (by subbing them out right away). Call out, "*Next!*" then have faith and be patient.

Soon, you will have players who are not only fearless of failure but who also hustle to fix it. Instead of tossing arms in the air, crying out, and trudging back to the sidelines or bench, they hustle to get to the *next* opportunity so they can get it right. This is a sight to behold when you have an entire team of players hustling for the *next* ball.

Peril Words—Words that Shut Down Peak Performance

Chapter 12

DON'T

When we encourage children to take risks at young ages, they build up problem-solving skills and learn to analyze their own game, creating internal feedback structures. An athlete who can self-assess and provide herself feedback is a learner.

John Kessel, former director of sport for USA Volleyball, tells a story about his professional volleyball days. His team was playing a rival whom they had not beaten in seventeen years. Toward the end of the game, they were up 13–5.

They were on the verge of doing what had been thought impossible so far in their history (causing stress) against a team with whom emotions already ran high (causing more stress) in front of a hostile crowd (even more stress). The anxiety was getting to the players as the mentality shifted from "we got this" (confidence) to "I hope we don't choke" (doubt).

A teammate of John's served the ball directly into the net, giving away a free point. They won back the serve, only to have another teammate serve the ball right into the net as well. The players' nerves were fraying, and the coach became increasingly frustrated at this sudden "tightening" in their performance (instead of being loose and confident, they were playing tight and with fear).

They won serve, and then it was John's turn. Coach yelled out to him in a strong and demanding voice, "*Don't* serve the ball into the net!"

Instead of a serve, John promptly and intentionally threw the ball over his head, out of bounds, and deep into the stands behind him. John's team got the next two points and won the match anyway. It was a wild risk, but John had full confidence in his team.

Later, after celebrating the historic win and waiting for the hostile home crowd to disperse—a crowd decidedly unhappy about this loss—the coach asked John, "What did I say to you when you were serving?"

John replied, "I think you told me, 'Don't serve it into the net'."

His coach responded exasperatedly, "That is exactly what I told you!"

John calmly said, "I didn't. You see, Coach, you tell us all the time what *not to do*. I want my brain to be focused on what I *should do* because there are a billion things not to do. My brain doesn't want to know anything about the nots, it wants to know what I can do."

The following Monday, John's coach stopped using *don't* and started coaching the players on what he wanted them *to do* instead.

It's usually not acceptable for players to directly disobey their coaches—or to hit a ball so blatantly out of bounds—but John had made his point in multiple ways. The coach was mature enough and smart enough to learn the valuable lesson about the significance of words.

Don't Increases Anxiety

Don't is a peril word. It causes a series of triggers in the brain that have no good use in the performance space. When coaches are constantly telling their players *don't*, many things happen in the minds of their players.

First, player creativity and risk behaviors are stifled. Experts advocate regularly for coaches to cultivate creativity in sports and encourage high-risk behaviors. The more play steered into sports and the more freedom athletes have to develop, the better the development curve. Science points to fun maps, play processes, and elite-level athletes who display phenomenal problem-solving and creativity as examples of what happens when we allow children to play in a "safe to fail" environment. When we allow children to explore, it builds resilience to failure, as they will fail often through trial and error but learn to self-correct and overcome adversity.

When we permit freedom, children will gain confidence from playing without consequences for any mistakes while trying new things. They will be confident to try again and become even more creative.

When we encourage children to take risks at young ages, they build up problem-solving skills and learn to analyze their own game, creating internal feedback structures. An athlete who can self-assess and provide herself feedback is a learner. A grower. These are the athletes who set their own development pace and will accept feedback from others.

The problem with the word *don't* is it shuts down all of the aforementioned opportunities. A child stops trying if every avenue of exploration is shut down for them. It's like trying to find their way out of a thick and confusing maze. Every turn the child takes, an adult says, "Don't go that way." Soon, there are no turns left for the child to take. And he stops trying. He doesn't risk another turn; he doesn't get creative with how to escape the maze.

Ironically, it's this moment when the child (or athlete) is inches from the solution, but we "don'ted" them into no more attempts.

Second, *don't* is one of the words the brain can easily filter, like a filler word. We know the basic premise for speed reading is to cut out the filler words as you go. The mind will fill them in while comprehending the surrounding text. As you scan a page, you mostly look for verbs and nouns, allowing the brain to fill in the adjectives, pronouns, and conjunctions. The more adept you get at this, the faster and more easily the brain filters out all of those "unnecessary" words. For example, you might scan over a sentence and comprehend, "Tom shot ball hoop cheered." You get the gist of the sentence from those words alone. *Tom scored.* The full sentence may have read, "Tom nervously shot the orange, round, heavy ball from thirty feet away into the circular hoop, and the expecting crowd cheered wildly."

You didn't need all the fluff. Your brain simply filtered it to make reading it faster and easier. All you need is basic information and an ability to comprehend. Broca's and Wernicke's areas had enough information to help you process (in this case Broca more so than Wernicke, as it is the seat for 'read' language).

So imagine if your mind simply filters *don't*. It is not proper; it may be a glitch in the software, but it can happen. When the mind is tense, stress is high, the game is on the line, and the mind tries to process at a million miles an hour under duress, it could filter the wrong word.

Recall golfer Jean Van de Velde in the 1999 British Open at Carnoustie. Going into the eighteenth hole, he could make double bogey and still bring home the Claret Jug. He had six strokes to give. After a risky tee shot had him at the edge of Barry Burn, he had only 185 yards to make five shots, but the wheels fell off of his victory bus.

He slammed his next shot into the stands, the ball ricocheting off of a rock wall and landing in thick grass back near Barry Burn. He chunked the next shot right into—you guessed it—Barry Burn. His next shot went into a green-side bunker. He finished the hole with a seven, and it is considered one of the most epic final hole meltdowns in professional golf (I have to say professional because I have had far better meltdowns in my amateur golf career).

What was he thinking? People ask that all of the time as they review and question his shot selection, mentality, and approach to the hole.

Van de Velde took it all in stride, noting that it is easy to win with grace but far more difficult to lose with grace. He has never said what he was thinking . . . only that he played it right and did the best he could.

But *what was he thinking?* Could his mind have been saying, "*Don't* pull it into the bleachers"? Oops.

"Don't hit it in Barry Burn." Oops.

"Okay, don't hit that darned bunker by the green." Oops. Oops. Oops.

In pressure situations, when we are being told *don't* or when we are telling ourselves *don't*, our minds could very well be filtering the *don't* right out of the sentence.

Did Van de Velde's psyche hear, "Pull it into the bleachers" right before impact, and the neurons fired so the muscles did just that? Did it then say, "Hit the Barry Burn"? Done. "Hit that darned bunker by the green"? Copy that.

> **The brain visualizes language, and certain words like "don't" have no visual representation. That means if you say, "Don't trip," all the brain can visualize is "trip."**

He is an elite-level athlete. John Kessel and his teammates were elite-level athletes. They hit the net twice, and who knows if John would have hit it had he listened to his coach. They train under pressure, prepare for the pressure, and expect that kind of pressure. So what gives?

What about those athletes who are not elite yet? Do we typically provide sports psychologists to our young athletes to help them develop pre-performance routines, reset protocols in moments of meltdown, or build mental resilience? No.

Do we train them in ways that armor them against having such moments? No. Many coaches and clubs don't have the budget or training to provide this type of resource to their athletes. We hope we are building some sort of resilience through our training programs and our words. We hope the culture we create allows them to overcome these moments or not fall into traps with them, but we can make no guarantees.

Let's look at our amateur sporting careers, our weekend warrior escapades. Do you have a staff psychologist to help you prepare for golfing with your buddies on Sundays? Do you train all week in pressure situations and put yourself in impossible "two-minute-like" drills to build resilience, calm, and focus, in case you are standing over a three-foot win-it-all putt on Sunday?

Try this the next time you play with your buddy, if he is one of those guys whose emotions can run high and he loses focus or if she is one of those athletes that spends too much time in her head and out-thinks herself. When they are standing over a very short putt or looking at a prominent hazard that is definitely in play, increase the stakes. Make a bet that gets the butterflies going a little. Talk up the odds and the dangers. Really stoke the anxiety fire.

Then, right before the shot, say, "Hey. You got this. Just don't miss the putt" or "Don't hit it in the water." See what happens. Your partner may have done that seven times out of ten anyway, but you certainly increased the odds by raising the stakes and adding in that bomb of a sentence, which the mind undoubtedly will change to, "Miss the putt."

Another peril of the word *don't* is that it can focus the mind on the negative. The athlete's mindset at the young or novice level can be quite fragile. They are navigating a lot of environmental stimuli and mental pressure to learn, perform, socialize, and not look silly.

Add the fact that the coach is constantly telling the athletes, "*Don't* do this, and *don't* do that," and we create negativity. This negativity can cause stress reactions in athletes, which secrete hormones detrimental to performance, raise anxiety levels, and promote the creation of additional negative thoughts all on their own.

Think about our athletes as flower gardens, and our words are either bulbs or bombs. We can grow beautiful flowers with the bulbs we plant or destroy the entire landscape with the bombs we drop. It is our choice. The words we use as coaches will become the words they also choose to use. Our dialogue will become their inner monologue—the voice they hear when they perform.

Do we want to be *don'ting* on them all of the time? Not a chance. We want to land bulbs with words that provide positive feedback and show them what they can do, as we direct them toward creativity, risk-taking, and growth.

To do this, we have to eliminate the peril word *don't* and give them, as John Kessel said, "The variance in this area that is okay." In other words, the options they can try and should try.

Instead of, "*Don't* serve into the net," what if his coach had said, "Hit it backcourt"? What if instead of telling your athletes *don't,* you could give them the gift of *do* and open their minds to the full spectrum of what is possible in sports.

Back to the maze analogy: If you eliminate *don't,* instead of shutting down all avenues of escape from the maze, you might elevate your athletes so they can see the entire maze from above and be able to map out their options for solving it.

Chapter 13

TRY

———◆———

*I'll try is the language of doubt, and doubt
is a development destroyer.*

"Hey, Dad?" My son yelled over the din of the hockey crowd.

"Yeah, Coop . . ." I responded, not allowing my eyes to leave the ice.

"We getting ice cream after the game?"

We were doing our usual Friday night out on the town. Dinner, a Miami Hockey game, and some quality dude time.

This was a tradition in our family—a way I connected with my kids. We had gotten lucky back in the summer when season ticket renewals came up and a friend didn't want a pair of his anymore. We didn't have the money, but we scraped together enough to buy them.

I had grown up going to Miami hockey games since I could recall. My mom tells the story of being nine months pregnant with me at a game, primed to give birth at any moment. When I was in graduate school, I lived with one of the team's graduate assistants and hung out with the team and staff. The "old Goggin" caused my wife to go into labor with our middle child. She was walking the tall, long steps of the rink while our daughter took skating lessons. Later that night, we had our second child.

Needless to say, the family legacy of Miami hockey runs deep and was part of who we were. We lived in town, everyone went to the games, and since I coached at the small, local high school, we knew everyone there. It was your typical Midwest event where everyone goes to the games to see and be seen and then talk about it the next Monday.

For our family, it meant one-on-one time with Dad. For each home game, I would rotate through whose turn it was to go to a game with me, and we would make a fun night of it.

This season, the pre-bought tickets made it a little more financially doable, but I was also in graduate school (a second time, who goes to graduate school twice? Especially at thirty-eight years old?) Money was tight on the babysitting and serving salary my wife fetched and the student loans and soccer coaching I pieced together. My poor wife didn't even get to go to the games because her best tip nights were Fridays and Saturdays, and she was only working for the sake of the family.

When You're Too Broke For Ice Cream

On this particular night, we were flat broke. I wasn't due to get my check from my soccer club for another week, and they were notoriously late with sending them. I knew it would be at least ten days before we had money to put in our account. The next week, we'd be about living off whatever my wife made at Buffalo Wild Wings and through childcare. My wife is such a hero that two of the kids she cared for had been attending for free for a year to help their parents get out of money issues.

There was no money in our account—the only money to our name was what I had brought with me to the game. I bought us dinner and, of course, hot drinks at the game (another part of the tradition). My son got his regular hot chocolate, and I drank my coffee. I had kept aside just enough to go get dessert after the game. This was also part of the tradition. When I was a kid, we would walk over to the student union after hockey games to get "toasted buns." It was some folklore "Miami Res" treat and was exactly what it sounded like. A toasted butter bun, smeared with peanut butter, and topped with powdered sugar and a scoop of ice cream. Every time I had one, memories of childhood came flooding back, and I wanted nothing more than to create those kinds of memories for my children.

Toasted buns were not much of a thing at this time. Most employees had never heard of them, so we had to help them make it every time we ordered them, and, sadly, they were not as much a hit with my kids. We usually opted for ice cream uptown and "student watching" (or "walkers" as my one son called them because they reminded him of the walkers in *The Walking Dead*—stumbling, making weird noises, and in search of food.)

On this night, however, we had accidentally spilled our neighbor's drink during the second intermission, and I offered to replace it. That was the last of our cash for the night. The cupboard was dry. I had nothing for ice cream and couldn't admit to my son that I was broke. *What would he think of his dad?*

"We'll try," I answered, trying to act unshaded, hoping he would drop it.

"Oh, OK," he said, sounding disappointed.

"Why do you sound that way?"

"That's what adults say when they don't want to say no but aren't going to do it," he responded firmly and matter-of-factly.

My heart sank. I couldn't believe what he had just said to me! He had nailed his assessment, but worse, he could predict my actions based on what I thought were simple words. My simple response, meant to delay the inevitable, hoping he would later forget, actually gave him a complete and final answer.

Try Promotes Doubt

That moment has always stuck with me. Every time I answer someone with "try", I wonder if they think what my son thought that night. I wonder if they know what is going on in my head. I wonder if I will disappoint them as much as I did my son. I know when I hear "try," I now expect the worst because *try* is a cop-out of sorts.

Try is an escape word—a word used to evade the original ask. The person using *try* is hoping to delay until they come up with a better excuse for saying no. The person using try is not very interested but doesn't want to admit it. They have better things to do, don't have the time or money, or would rather do something else, but it seems too harsh to say no.

Instead of being honest and admitting the enormous elephant in the room, many people just respond with *try*. When your friend asks you to come to his piano recital because he took up piano two weeks ago at forty-eight years old, and you can't possibly imagine subjecting your ears to what may transpire, you say, "I'll try."

When your best friend wants to set you up with another friend of hers and you simply don't want to be dating anyone right now, you say, "Let me try to find a night that might work."

When your boss asks if you would have time to come in on Saturday for some unpaid work, you say, "I can try to rearrange my busy schedule."

> **It's not what you say, it's what they hear.**
> **When you say, "I'll try," they hear,**
> **"It's not worth the effort".**

You get it. *Try* is a much better way to evade the offer. To push it off in the hopes of something better or until you can figure out a better excuse. *Try* is also a word that permits people to fall short of a goal without feeling the "burn" of missing it. If you are not sure whether you can accomplish something but don't want to admit it, or don't want to look like a fool, you simply say, "Try." It is akin to saying, "This is really tough and out of my zone, but I will give my best, and when I fall short, you will know it wasn't for lack of skill; it was simply too much."

Like when my son asked me to do one hundred straight push-ups one time, and I knew 50–75 would probably be pushing it well beyond my limit, I didn't want him to know that. So I said "Well, that is quite an ask. It would take a real beast to do it, but I can certainly try." Then, I don't look a fool when I can't make it halfway there. It was tough, and I gave it my best.

Try is also a promoter of doubt. The moment the word is spoken, doubt slowly rolls across the brains of all who hear it, like a low rolling mist off of the ocean at night. It covers everything in a hazy uncertainty. Outcomes become hard to see, and it's hard to get our bearings and know what is out there. There is a reason Stephen King wrote a horror novel about the mist. It is a scary place of uncertainty. So is the word *try.*

When you are teaching a child a complex skill, and she says, "I'll try," she is telling you she doubts her abilities, doesn't understand what you are teaching, and possibly needs more help. She is confirming in her mind how difficult the task will be. Even if she was close to accomplishing the skill, the moment *try* crosses her lips, the mist of doubt grips her brain tightly, taking away any confidence she had in herself beforehand.

Try is evasion. It is doubt; it is an excuse, and it is a word of peril that sets everyone involved up for disappointment. *Try* is a word that needs to be eliminated from the performance arena. Its use has become synonymous with excuses and shortfalls. Its legacy is one of misgiving. It is time to break up with *try* and date a happier word. We don't need that kind of negativity in our lives.

We must help our players eliminate doubt from their psychological profile because it is a lethal weapon against development. Doubt is easy to fall victim to, and therefore, we must be vigilant about the words that create it. First and foremost, *try* is the king of the doubt words. So let's start there. Banish the king, and maybe we banish them all.

To help athletes remove the word *try* from their vocabulary, you must model what you want. You are no longer allowed to dismiss players with a simple, "I'll try." You either say yes or no and be honest with them about your intentions. Athletes want honest coaches and can quickly read *try* as a byproduct of inauthenticity. Seriously, my eight-year-old son figured it out fairly easily. Your athletes know. Not only is it disconnecting you from them, but it is also teaching them it is okay for them to break promises or dismiss people with a half-butted answer. They will let you and their teammates down because *try* was a learned way to do it.

Second, redirect their *try* responses. When an athlete says, "I don't know, Coach. I'll try," before the sentence is finished, you need to replace the word with *will*, *can*, or *commit*. You simply tell your athlete, "You mean, I [will/can/commit to it]?" This sets the responsibility back on your athlete, steels their resolve, and gives them full ownership of the process. It is not out of their control, something too hard to do, or something they may be incapable of. It is simply a commitment for them to work toward, no matter the length of time it takes. It is a promise to oneself to avoid quitting or copping out, and, instead, be resilient.

Finally, change how you ask things of athletes. Instead of asking them to do things for you, teach them to want to do things for themselves and their team. If you are constantly saying, "I want you to do this," it is not theirs to want but yours. They are merely doing something for someone else and *try* is such an easy response to use to hide behind a lack of ownership or motivation. If you compel them to want to do it by tapping that competitive nerve, empowering them to have ownership in the learning process, or by asking more questions, *try* will be removed from consideration.

Imagine asking an athlete what they think about a situation. Asking what they would do to solve the problem. What it would look like if they did solve it? Then you said to the athlete, "Do it." You have allowed the athlete to develop the solution, visualize the result, and decide on action. Now, you are not ordering an athlete to bid your doing, you are compelling someone who has already decided to "get on with it." Nike was onto something with their slogan, "Just do it."

Imagine also a culture that puts players first, cultivates a sense of responsibility within the team, and instills a desire to seek everyday excellence. This kind of team doesn't even recognize *try* as a response option. The options become either do it or pass it on to someone who can—like Steph Curry in the 2017 NBA Finals. His teammate, Kevin Durant, had the hot hand. Steph knew someone needed to take the reins and score the needed points. His resolve was not to *try* himself. He got the ball to the man who could. He passed to Kevin, then set picks for him! Steph Curry has no idea what *try* means. He knows *will* and *can*. He knows if he is not the guy, he won't try haphazardly, he will empower the guy who can to do it. Of course, next time, he may just be the guy because he also knows the words *yet* and *now*, words that remind him everything is temporary. Tomorrow, or the *next* time, he will have the hot hand and be ready for the call. This is the power of turning try into *will*, *can*, or *commit*.

The next time you want to take the easy road and use *try*, be willing to challenge yourself and be brutally honest and resolute. Either admit you don't want to or have other plans or boldly claim *you will*.

Chapter 14

NEVER

*Tell someone they can't, and they will
want to do it more than ever.*

His nickname was "The Experiment," and he never lost. Many believe he was called that because he was so implausible as a human wrestler that he had to have been cooked up in some dank, darkly lit lab miles beneath the frozen tundra of Siberia. He has also been called the "Russian Bear" and "Russian King Kong." Those nicknames invited a wave of fear washing over anyone asked to step into a wrestling ring with him.

He was a massive man, standing six-foot-four and weighing over 290 pounds in his prime. Besides size, he had brute strength. Known for training in the waist-deep snow of Eastern Russia, then rowing a boat until his hands bled, and benching 450 pounds a day as part of a regimen to build pure strength. His opponents didn't understand him because, as he said, "I used to train every day like they never had in their lives."

He was feared. He recounted to one reporter that he saw that fear in his opponents' eyes because "no one wanted to fly." Of course, he was referring to his patented move, the Karelin Lift (named after him), in which he would grab his 300-pound opponent and toss him head-over-heels back down to the mat (Google the Karelin Lift and then prepare to not sleep for days).

His opponents also feared him because he had only lost twice in 289 matches. Two-hundred eighty-seven wins. Most were by pin because his opponents would rather give up than be thrown into orbit and slammed back down on the unforgiving wrestling mat. He never met an opponent he feared. He claims his toughest opponent was a refrigerator weighing nearly twice as much as him. His parents bought it but couldn't get it up the eight flights of stairs to the apartment, so, according to legend and Karelin himself, he bear-hugged it, hoisted it, and walked it up the eight flights on his own.

If that story didn't make him the most feared athlete in the world in 2000, his international record should have. He had not lost in thirteen years, had only conceded one solitary point in ten years, and was riding three straight gold medals. The only loss in his career occurred during the 1987 USSR Championships, where he fell to reigning World Champion Igor Rostorotsky, whom he promptly defeated at the next USSR Championships.

Headed into the Sydney Games, his fourth gold medal was all but an afterthought. He was a lock to win it. When the games panned out and an unknown Wyoming farm boy, who had never placed higher than fifth in an international competition, was his opponent in the finals, it seemed the medal was his, save the ceremony.

"This Wyoming kid, named Rulon Gardner, will never defeat Karelin." Many said as much, and many more believed it. The Experiment had beaten—boldly and astoundingly—every man who stepped in the ring with him, and Rulon would never stand a chance. They had met once before, and Karelin used his famous lift to slam Rulon, like a rag doll, to the mat.

But what transpired was the stuff of athletic fairy tales. The perfect plot for a Hollywood feel-good sports movie. The unknown and untested underdog against the freak of nature, who had never lost. A true David and Goliath matchup, equal to the famous Miracle on Ice of Lake Placid in 1980. Rulon had never heard the word *never*, and Alexander Karelin never saw him coming.

Rulon Gardner got his single point by keeping The Experiment from ever getting the leverage to throw him and breaking a clinch hold at the beginning of the second round. He matched strength for strength, strategy for strategy, and agility with agility. In the end, Alexander Karelin was so stunned by this unbelievable moment, he dropped his hands to indicate defeat with eight seconds left. He then removed his shoes and walked off, leaving behind the sport forever. (In wrestling, leaving your shoes on the mat indicates retirement.)

Rulon Gardner became the unlikely American hero, and Alexander Karelin walked away from the sport he had dominated for thirteen years. Though, he is still considered the greatest Greco-Roman wrestler of all time. Rulon is the man who refused to understand the absolute of a word like *never*.

Never is a word we should rarely use, especially in an unpredictable realm like sports. *Never* is an absolute. It means at no time in the past or the future . . . on no occasion, not ever. It is far too absolute a word to be used in a setting where underdogs and upsets exist, like in entrepreneurship, sports, or politics. The massively favored have to work just as hard every day to remain favorites as the underdogs work to unseat them. *Never* is an absolute the underdog wishes to hear as a motivator and the favorites fear hearing as an omen of danger.

Never is also a word that gives away power, reduces risk-taking, and potentially causes what is called a "backlash effect." When we use the word *never*, we are entering a perilous situation because it limits the performance or has an alternate effect on the expected outcome.

When we tell performers to *never* do something, for instance, we are stealing their power to choose. In sales, in high-performance environments, and in sports, we require those we lead to be flexible and autonomous enough to make instant decisions. We train them on all possible scenarios; we prepare them to face stressful situations with a "blue head," and then we coach them to make the best possible choices to ensure the intended outcome (commander's intent). When we use a word like *never*, we take that power. We reduce the options, allowing an absolute to dictate where absolutes don't exist. There are too many variables to uphold a *never*.

For instance, in soccer, I have heard coaches of young players say, "Never play the ball across our own goal" or "Never play the ball backward"; yet, this is not simply a variable but a norm at the higher levels. Nearly every world-class team plays the ball across its own goal and plays the ball backward. At its core, soccer is a possession game. Keep the ball and you can score. Keep the ball and your opponent cannot score. Why would we tell players to *never* do something that might allow them to keep the ball (passing across the field or back to an open teammate)?

We know at young ages, the opportunity to mess up is higher. We want to reduce the mistakes of giving up easy goals to the opponent, and thus, we tell them never to do those two things. But an absolute like *never* allows people, especially children, to solve only part of the puzzle. The *never* option is closed, making fewer options available to consider. The danger is that we have reduced their power to choose. The next time they come across a questionable decision, they look to us for the answer instead of utilizing one of the best resources we have available for learning: trial and error toward discovery.

Never also reduces risk-taking. Again, it is a word fraught with finality. An absolute that eases the stress of having to "run scenarios" in the brain. We like tidy, efficient answers. When we are told something like "electric cars will never be feasible as a transportation option," it gives us another option to check off on a long list of options. It makes our decision tree easier to manage. It also reduces our risky behaviors. We won't consider an electric car because of the absolute finality of that statement. *Never* tells us to avoid the risk on a specific route.

Finally, *never* can produce a "backfire effect," as in the case of The Miracle on Ice or the Miracle on the Mat (as the Rulon Gardner victory was termed). When we tell someone *never*, we hope to dissuade the person from making a certain choice, but we may motivate them to be more committed to that choice.

> **Never is a fatal word. It halts all progress as we focus on the problems and the impossibility. The key is to develop a problem-aware and solution-focused mindset that removes never from the narrative and encourages forward motion. See it. Solve it.**

We discussed earlier the phenomenon of the mind removing the word *don't* from statements. The brain does the same with *never*. A person hearing "never" may simply hear the entire sentence minus the *never* and carry on with what we were attempting to prevent.

Never strengthens some people's resolve. Telling a largely outmatched underdog that she will never win may only steel her willpower. It might give her greater courage and a more virulent belief in her ability to do the task.

This sometimes happens because, like confirmation bias, our minds unconsciously and instinctively defend our beliefs against "attitude-in-consistent" information. In other words, telling someone *never* when they believe the opposite will cause a backfire. They will believe even more strongly in what we contradict. Rulon faced a plain fact: no one could beat Karelin. Add to it the fact that he marched, nearly unopposed, to the finals at the 2000 Olympic Games and had only been scored on once in the last ten years. The word *never* was being shouted from all directions.

But Rulon had faith. He had courage. He had nothing to lose, so hearing *never* caused a backfire effect. Instead of caving to the demands of the critics around him, giving in to the belief that the gold medal was Karelin's, Rulon took a more Spartan attitude. When Xerxes told the Spartans he would darken the sky with arrows, they said they would "fight in the shade." Tell me *I can't*, and I now want to do it more than ever.

We should avoid *never* when working with our teams. We cannot afford to cut off options when the very nature of what we teach is about analyzing options and learning the best methods. We should not seek to take power from our teams when our goal is to create new leaders (this should be a goal of any leader—leaders create leaders), and we certainly do not want to risk uttering an absolute to a competitor and unleashing the backlash effect.

Never is typically used in some form of a feedback environment. To avoid using *never* in this situation, try:

1. Providing specific information with details and asking for a different solution. Instead of telling a player to never do something, explain what it was he did, what the intended outcome was versus the actual outcome, why it may not have been an ideal choice, and then ask if they can think of a better solution.

2. When discouraging an action, be honest and context-specific. Tell your team member why the action was unacceptable based on standards the team has developed; ask if they know how

others affected by the action may have felt, and ask if this is the kind of teammate they desire to be. Providing this kind of honest and context-specific feedback gives the team members some perspective. It provides a framework for better understanding in the moment and with future decision-making.

3. Ask more questions and encourage alternative solutions. Do not shut down risk-taking or analysis with an absolute like *never*; instead, ask the person what happened—what was different that provided the undesired outcome and what alternative solutions might be.

4. Provide context around the situation. I don't enjoy telling athletes to *never* try a skill, but I feel it is important to tell them when and where a skill is best served. Giving them context allows them to know the skill is useful and permits them to use it, but context also provides a time and place for when it is most effective. This will help them consider not using it in the current context again.

5. Eliminate *never* from motivational conversations. For the favorites, it promotes a sense of overconfidence and can lead to laziness. A team that thinks they can never be beaten will "take their foot off the gas" just long enough to be beaten. Could that have happened to Karelin? Did he let up just enough at that moment to have his grip broken, thus giving away the only point of the match?

We may *never* know the answer.

Chapter 15

BUT

"But" is a word that crushes dreams, dashes hope, stops journeys, and demotivates even the most faithful people.

"You are one heck of a player. You have great ball-handling skills, good range on your shots, and are quick on defense. Not to mention you see passes and holes in the defense that no one else sees, and you are one of the quickest defenders I've seen in a long time. There is no doubt you can play. You are also a witty kid; the other kids like you, and you are a natural leader. Your attributes coupled with your skill means you can ball, but . . ."

But Is the Stinky Part of the Conversation

There it was. The word that would unravel a short but fun basketball career. The word that would obliterate any hopes or deeds before its utterance. My mind went blank, like retrograde amnesia, at the sound of the word *but* as I became hyper-focused on what was said next.

". . . you are a bit cocky, and I feel you have a bit of an attitude. You may be skilled and be a leader, but I need coachable kids. So I'm cutting you."

It was a long and silent car ride home. It's not that I didn't want to speak. I couldn't speak. I was both devastated and totally confused. I had just been cut from the freshman basketball team. A team all of my former teammates from the top AAU teams in Southern Ohio made. I had been one of the top basketball players in the city since sixth grade. All my old teammates from middle school who were not at this high school would start varsity as freshmen at my hometown high school. And I had been cut. This tryout should have been, as voiced by many of my fellow participants, "a shoo-in" for me. Everyone, including me, expected I would be the starting point guard for the freshman team.

I was a starter, captain, and leading scorer on the freshman soccer team. I was a former starter and captain of my middle school basketball team, one that had only lost three times in sixty games over the last two years. I was a starter and captain—and leading scorer—of my middle school football team. I was also a starter and leader of the City Champion Cheviot Fire AAU team. I was ultra-confident going into tryouts. I was also insecure about quite a few things and hid those insecurities by being the funny man—overly social.

During tryouts, there were a few times I should have toned down my humor. There were more than a couple of instances where I was talking when I should have been paying better attention. There were also times I talked smack to my teammates during scrimmages, purely out of "boys being boys" fun (or so I thought).

I also bucked authority. When Coach wanted me to go skins, I refused. I had terrible acne on my chest—cystic acne that had left deep scars. I was painfully self-conscious of the stares and comments I might get when I took off my shirt. To this day, I am not big on going shirtless. What seems like a normal and quite inane thing to most guys (taking off their shirts) is a massive undertaking for me. I hem and haw. I deflect; I try to convince people otherwise, and I find a way to gracefully bow out of the situation. It is psychological anguish for me to go shirtless. I tried to overcome it in my mid-twenties by lifting weights and building a lot of upper body muscle, but it only worked for a few years.

You can imagine how a fourteen-year-old boy, already self-conscious and trying to fit in, would react when told he had to "go skins." The anxiety removed any modicum of tact. Instead, I tried to evade it, and when that didn't work, I bluntly refused. When pressured, I lost my cool, couldn't think straight, and, therefore, said "I don't want to." It came off as me being uncoachable, uncaring, stubborn, and cocky.

In his eyes, and Coach was not wrong, I had an attitude. I was overconfident. I was hiding how I really felt . . . but how could he have known all that? My witty banter and confidence hid the typical teenage nerves, and my blunt refusal to play "skins" belied a greater issue than attitude, but to the outside observer, it was simple obstinance.

Finally, my mother asked what happened. I told her, still numb.

"I got cut."

She steadied her response. There was surprise and disappointment, but my parents had always been supporters from a distance. They wanted us to play sports and succeed, but they also knew the deeper value of sports, so they remained hands-off in the affairs of our sporting careers.

"Why? Did he say why?"

"I have a bad attitude, and I'm cocky."

She prodded me for more information, but I had no recollection of anything else he said. The words he had spoken before "but" eluded me. Everything leading up to that word had been erased from existence with that simple three-letter conjunction. All of the compliments, the nice words, and the positive feedback were eliminated; all that remained were the negatives. I am cocky and have a bad attitude. I am not coachable.

But is the stinky part of a conversation. It is the conjunction that creates opposition between what was said before and after it. It is the undoing of what had already been done. It has a finality to it like the last word of a fight. Once it is spoken, the conversation dies, and usually what was said before it becomes the victim.

But is stinky because it is a word typically used to deliver stinky news, to lob negativity, or to shut down hope. It is stinky because what follows that word usually stinks to the listener.

"You are a great guy, but . . ."

"You've had a good run on this show, but . . ."

"It's an impressive resume, but . . ."

"We searched everywhere for your dog, but . . ."

"Doctors did all they could, but . . ."

None of these sentences end in happiness or positive outcomes. No one starts a sentence like "You have an impressive resume, but . . ." and ends it with ". . . we decided to hire you as the CEO instead of a junior sales leader." *But* crushes dreams, dashes hope, stops journeys, and demotivates even the most faithful people. *But* stinks.

Not only does it bring about a bad ending to a conversation, it can psychologically undo all that was done before it was spoken. Think about the sentence "You're a great guy, but . . ."

The figurative guy in the sentence may have had dreams of marriage, of life ever after. He was filled with love, happiness, and contentment. He thought highly of the object of his affection and also of himself for having been able to "make such a catch." This is all conjecture, but we can assume there were great memories made, deep feelings developed, and strong bonds formed. The word *but* undoes every single one. He will take a long time to look back with fondness on the memories. The more attached he was to this individual, the longer it will take to see the good and the more bitter he will be. All the good memories, dreams, and nice feelings and thoughts are immediately replaced with things like sadness, dolor, bitterness, longing, and maybe anger. All that was done is undone by *but*.

> **But is the stinkiest part of a conversation because everything said before it is lost in the stench of what is said after it.**

But also demotivates performance by providing excuses and shifting blame away from the only thing an athlete has control of—their performance. Have you ever heard an athlete say, "I would have won, but the referee was awful." This is not taking responsibility for the things an athlete can control. We cannot control the refs, the weather, or the bounce of the ball. We can control our preparation, performance, and reactions to the result. Using *but* demotivates us to be introspective about the role we took in not achieving the outcome we desired. Athletes who have *buts* have stinky attitudes.

It is not all their fault. We teach them this as adults when we also blame external factors or we never accept any responsibility for the role we play in losses. Coaches lose games when athletes lose games, yet we always tell them what they did wrong and then punish them with early morning "character runs" so it never happens again. I know I did that and never once ran with them.

If you want to eliminate the *but* as a way to shirk ownership, teach athletes to follow *but* with a positive.

"We would have won, but we learned a valuable lesson about playing in wet conditions."

"That was not the result I wanted, but the season is long, and I will get more chances to perform better."

This type of response is so much more powerful than blame-shifting.

The basketball career I had up to the moment I was cut disappeared after the *but*. I never played organized basketball again. I decided I was not good enough. I didn't want to hear any of the nice things the coach had said; all I could focus on was the negative that came after the *but*. All that had been done was undone.

This is an extreme example. I was a resilient athlete in many other areas and overcame many setbacks in my career. I was never good at sales, though, because I didn't like being told no.

Buts are Nos

I took the nos personally, and they shut me down immediately. I am not alone in this. Many people struggle to sell, which is why there are so many people and organizations making good money trying to teach the rest of us this highly coveted skill.

As humans, we crave connection and belonging. Being told no seems to sever a connection. We fear *no* because it means the absence of connection. At any level, *no* cuts ties. *But* is a variation on no. It usually precedes a version of no to us. *But* is the knife that severs the ties. It slices down between the moments leading up to it and separates all that comes after so that the only thing that remains is the no—the separation.

As a conjunction in grammar, *but* is used to separate one part of a sentence from another. The conjunction *and* combines and connects, but the stinky conjunction *but* separates.

This is what *but* did for me. It separated my short basketball career from a future in basketball, and for a while, I had no good memories, no momentum, and no recollection of the skill I had. I simply didn't feel I could play. After all, I was cocky and uncoachable. Fortunately, a word like *but* didn't drive me to think that about all areas of my life. Only basketball was affected by it.

As a leader, think of the times you have used *but* with your charges. Was it to deliver bad news? Or to provide negative feedback after positive feedback? Or was it to say no to a request of some kind?

We think that by crafting a sentence with positives first and negatives second, we can "let people down more easily" or add a silver lining. We are taught to be gentle by telling people good stuff and then following with the negative. We can ease them into the bad if we lead up with positives, but it only serves to accentuate the negative. *But* becomes the loudest word in the sentence and punches out the negative comment, just as all capital and bold letters would in written language. The first part of the sentence is forgotten. Only the *but* remains.

Worse, we have been taught to provide feedback sandwiches to people. Tell them something good, provide "constructive feedback," and then tell them something good again. Here is the thing about most "construction" projects: they are costly, messy, noisy, never timed well, and become eyesores until they are complete. So it stands to reason that the constructive feedback after the *but* is messy, noisy, costly, poorly timed, and not very pretty on the eyes. It is the only part of the sentence anyone focuses on because the word *but* punched it out so boldly. Even the "nice things" that come after the *but* are not well received because *but* separates the sentence into two parts: the positive and the negative. Even if another positive came after the conjunction, the negative was the loudest, messiest, most costly part of the sentence. Feedback sandwiches do not always work because of the stinky *but* in the middle of it all.

We can still provide feedback; we can still deliver bad news, and we can still turn down requests without putting our stinky *buts* in the conversation.

First, feedback should be a continual and organic process. Just as skill development and tactical development are "baked into" the learning process and seen as organic elements that we help guide as practitioners, so is feedback. If you are creating learning environments and cultures of excellence based on real talent development, then you are putting athletes in situations where they will get out of their comfort zones, analytical and honest enough to recognize what works and what doesn't, vulnerable enough to ask for help and admit when they are stuck, and confident and communicative enough to provide each other with feedback. In other words, you shouldn't have to save up feedback for singular moments away from the training ground or for end-of-season evaluations. It should be happening at all times through the learning process, through the way you communicate with them, and through the way they interact with each other. If you create the right environment, feedback exists as part of the environment.

When you need to provide feedback, you should have set a relationship with your athletes based on strong connection and trust, which means you do not need to "sugar coat" your words or beat around the bush with them. Be direct; tell them what you need to tell them, and then give them a chance to correct it. Athletes who trust their coaches expect feedback for growth. In addition, athletes who are connected with their coaches are willing to be guided through the process. Feedback does not need to be negative; it simply is feedback. It is part of the process, like a child navigating this new and wondrous world. The child tests everything, sometimes needing to be redirected, sometimes learning by trial and error, sometimes being told no lovingly and firmly.

Performers with a growth mindset crave feedback. They want it because their focus is solely on the process and mastery of the task or skill. Process and mastery behaviors require constant monitoring and feedback. People make fun of bodybuilders for staring at themselves in mirrors. Body-building requires precise muscle balance and focus on proper techniques to get the physique needed to win competitions. One slight variation in a technique could mean the difference between first and fourth place, or worse. The mirror watching is not out of an expanded ego; it is out of strict adherence to mastery. If we get our athletes or students focused on work ethic, process, and skill mastery, they, too, will seek that constant feedback, much like a bodybuilder who gazes into the mirror. Giving feedback doesn't need to be stinky if they are already seeking it.

Babies learn to walk through a process of trial and error that has constant feedback. They know when they know, yet when they become young athletes, we think we have to both joystick their every move and provide negative feedback. Instead, create environments where they can navigate trial-and-error patterns safely, with our guidance (not solutions), and then give the normal feedback you would to a baby. They learn by doing and by having the resilience to do it again with some feedback.

To avoid the *but,* don't use juxtaposing thoughts in the same sentence. Avoid having to say one thing and undo it with another. Say one thing. Period. You are delivering positive news or delivering negative news. If you have created a transformational relationship with your athletes in which you have connected with them and built trust, you don't need to let them down softly. Just tell them what you need to tell them. They trust you to have their best interests at heart, and they already know you care.

But sounds so impersonal. It tells the person you don't know them or you have been lying to them. Why say all the nice things to then undo it with *but?* It just feels so inauthentic. If you know your athletes and care about them, then just say what needs to be said without having to create falsehoods.

You can also eliminate the peril of *but* by changing the way you give feedback. Instead of being the sage on the stage, who always has to tell athletes the answers to the questions, like a professor who says, "Write this down. It will be on the test," try being a guide on their journey using questions of your own. You don't need to use *but* statements if they are the ones driving the conversation and you are merely helping move it along to their conclusion. How would that look? Much more Socratic than the current coaching model, that's for certain:

"How do you feel about that play?"

"What went well?"

"How could you do it differently?"

"Why did it happen?"

"What if you had another way to do it?"

"What would it look like, then?"

"How would you do that?"

"Are there any other options?"

The more you put the questions back on them, the more they grow in several key ways. First, they become analytical problem-solvers. This is a technique used by some of the world's greatest think tanks and also by the New Zealand All Blacks. The All Blacks place their athletes in highly stressful, uncomfortable situations, and then ask questions of them so they can solve the issues. If they can solve it in practice, they are more likely to be problem-solvers in the game when Coach cannot do the solving for them. They will be calm, stay focused, and think the issues through to a solution.

Second, you are empowering them to own their learning experience. You know the saying, "feed a man a fish . . ."? With our athletes, the more we give the answers, the more we are making them reliant on us in the future. If you want true development, the athletes have to be committed to it, bought into it, excited about it, and in control of it. This is done by putting the questions on them so you are "teaching them to fish" and they are developing their own answers. Athletes empowered through questions are the ones who are always seeking that 1 percent more of excellence every day, who are constantly working in the process and looking for opportunities at mastery. They work at practice and home because it is their learning—not your teaching—that matters.

Third, questions build resilience and motivation. Kids who have to seek answers realize that life is a puzzle. They don't shy from challenges but see a reward within the challenge itself. They are less outcome-focused and more effort-focused. They know their value is in seeking out challenges, being willing to stumble once in a while, but always giving their best effort. They know they can grow through hard work and persistence, like the children in Carol Dweck's research. They don't shut down when faced with setbacks or challenges but rise up to accept them regardless of the outcome. They are motivated to succeed through work and not by some innate "specialness" bestowed on them at birth. Your willingness to question them tells them it is okay to not have the answers, to not be instinctually good at something, because true magic lies in challenges. If all they ever got was "atta boys" or "you go, girls," they would never value the challenge. Because they are asked to think them through, the praise means nothing compared to the joy of seeking their own solutions.

One last way to eliminate the peril of *but* is to connect more deeply with your athletes. If you get to know them, if you invest in them, if you watch them and listen to them, then you know them well enough to know that all behaviors have underlying feelings. As the positive discipline saying goes, "You have to connect before you can correct." Taking the time to know your athletes avoids any misunderstandings. Knowing one of your kids is self-conscious about taking off his shirt means you never make him take it off and never have to tell him, "You are a good player, *but* you have an attitude."

This is not sour grapes because, honestly, soccer was my one true love as a sport, and it has given me so much. Besides, that experience gave me a story for better language in coaching. The clues were all there. I would grasp my shirt at my chest as long as I could. I would run to put it on at water breaks. The acne was so obvious, other kids made comments. I hinted at it in the "get to know you" portion of the first day when I said, "I have the worst farmer's tan known to man."

"Because you played soccer all summer?" someone asked.

"Yeah. That he never takes off his shirt," one of my former teammates stated in defense of me.

Knowing me would have probably eliminated the *but*. It's difficult to get to know kids in only a week or two of tryouts. I understand this, but if you watch them, listen to them, and see them, you learn a lot about them. When you know your athletes, you know enough about them to know what they can hear and cannot hear, how to speak to them, what their dreams and hopes are, how they best learn, what struggles they are facing, and what they need to succeed, *but* . . .

If you don't invest in them, you will never truly tap into their potential or do them justice. They will never develop the way they were meant to and you will have missed out on one of the best gifts of being a coach. It will end negatively, just like this conversation did after the *but*.

Chapter 16

WIN (COMPETE)

Celebrate wins with perspective. There's always more to learn.

"Dad, am I a disappointment?"

My son's question hit like a kick to the stomach. My family had just spent the day at a local amusement park. We hit all the best rides, ate junk food, enjoyed the summer weather, and laughed a lot. His comment was a complete surprise I had no words for a moment.

"No. Why would you ever think that?" I finally managed to respond.

"Because I am not a good soccer player and I don't like daredevil stuff like you." His tone was all business.

My heart broke at that moment. I was fighting back tears as I realized his concern was a direct result of the language I had used with him over the years. It is true my son doesn't like scary things. He refused to ride most of the roller coasters that day. He has been that way his entire life. I recalled the look of utter fear and the swift intake of breath through clenched teeth every time he rode a swing as a baby. My little guy was definitely "risk-averse."

The playing career is another story. I honestly could care less if he was a great athlete. I just wanted him to play so he could feel the joy and passion I did. I hoped he would have amazing coaches who built into him like mine did me. And I wanted him to play sports for the man he would become along the way, not for any awards he would get at the end.

He thought he was a failure in my eyes. He was concerned I didn't love him as much as I could because he wasn't a winner. He didn't score a lot of goals or play on high-level teams and wasn't going to extend some arbitrary and downright inane legacy in our family. He believed I was disappointed, and it was my fault.

Throughout my son's career, I had set him up to fail. I had planted seeds and set the processes in his brain that caused him to become hyper-focused on outcomes and not on the process. I did this with words—or more specifically, a single word, which I used all of the time.

"Win."

I missed quite a few of his games because I was off coaching other games or doing club-related stuff as the director of coaching and then as the executive director of a soccer club. I thought the damage would be in that I was not at enough of his games, but the damage grew out of the first thing I asked him after games.

"Did you win?" The next question I would ask is "Did you score?" I had set him up to worry only about outcomes with those questions. Worse, because I had a fairly good athletic career myself and many stories were told of my exploits (they get better every year), and also because I was a prolific goal scorer when I was young, he had created a measuring stick to which he thought he was measured. And the downstream assumptions just got worse. Win like Dad. Score a lot like Dad.

When Dad asks if you won or scored and you haven't, you are not like him. If you are not like Dad, he will be disappointed. You are a failure.

My goodness. Standing in that parking lot of the amusement park, this brilliant orange and blue sunset spilling across the sky like some painting from a museum behind us, I was faced with the very real nightmare of having made my son think I loved him less because of some silly sport. I couldn't help but start crying.

My son was quiet—stoic. He wasn't sure how to handle his father, now with tears running down his cheeks.

I tried to muster some kind of recovery. "Son, that was my path. That was my life. You are expected to walk your own path, and I love you for who you are . . . not what you do."

Good recovery, Reed. That will set him straight. All will be well.

"I know, but you like winning. You won a lot as a player and a coach. I just wanted to make you happy and do the same."

Punch. To. The. Gut. My son's words knocked the wind clear out of me. He had paid close attention to my life, to my words. He had built this entire existence around what I had said instead of what he wanted to do.

Win Obscures Objectives and Is Outcome-Orientated

It was never about winning for me. It was a byproduct of great coaching, a lot of hard work and mastery, and a second-to-none values system instilled by my mentors and coaches. Yes, I won, but I never seemed to be focused on that part until my college career. And that was, to be honest, one reason I didn't want to play anymore. My college coach was fanatical about winning. Everything was binary with him: win or lose. In training, at team dinners, and especially in the games. You were winning or you were failing. After we reached the national semi-finals my freshman year, the push to win was unbearable.

We went from experiencing joy and having fun, enjoying the game, to 5:00 a.m. training, mid-afternoon conditioning blocks, and evening practice sessions. He drove us as if we had something to prove every time we stepped on the field. We quickly burned out from all of it.

Coach yelled and screamed when things were not perfect. He would punish us with conditioning when we didn't win. He would pit us against each other. I recall "hating" one of my fellow teammates because Coach made us compete for everything, and to the winner went the spoils. The loser got the ridicule during the stretching circle.

During one game, I saw him destroy a medical kit by kicking it when our opponent scored. In another game, he threw a water jug and all of the cups onto the field. Win and he'd be all smiles and laughter. Lose and it was a scene from *The Exorcist*.

I didn't want that for my kids. I wanted them to have the joy I had growing up and the passion that kept me coaching the game. I never yelled at my sons. I never drove them so hard that they cried. Yet, my words did just enough to set them up to lose the love of the game, just like I did when I was twenty-one.

Win is a peril word. It obscures the real objectives of youth sports. It refocuses all involved on outcomes rather than on processes. Sports, like any other activity in a child's life, is about learning, developing new skills, being exposed to good values, and finding positive role models. It is ultimately about mastery and process, not winning and outcomes.

When we shift our focus to winning, as I did with my constant queries of my son, we shape the mindsets of our athletes—not in a good way. They cut corners to be first. They don't complain about a little cheating if it means getting the *W*. They think winning is the cure-all to everything. It will make all the pain go away.

Winning doesn't make the pain go away. It is more like a numbing agent. It masks the deeper problem so we can keep doing what we do, and in the long run, the damage morphs into something even worse.

When you numb an injury, for instance, and play through it, you risk making it worse. When you focus on winning at the expense of nobler objectives, you also risk a far worse outcome.

I am not against winning. I love to win. I am against a sole focus on winning at the expense of all the other (real) benefits of youth sports. When kids get trophies but cheat to get them or adults celebrate medals but teach poor values to get them, we have a problem. We have an obligation to teach our children the good things, such as sportsmanship, resiliency, respect, and integrity. Those values are endangered when our focus is only on the outcome. A win-at-all-costs mentality ignores the importance of such values.

Worse, our kids never learn the real meaning of competition if they are focused on winning. Competition comes from the Latin root word *competere*, which means to strive together. Striving together is more akin to iron sharpening iron than cheating to get the gold.

Our children should learn the value of hard work. They should know that losing is part of learning and is not fatal, but rather, a road sign on our journeys—just as winning is a road sign on our journeys. They should believe that facing tough challenges or tough opponents makes them stronger. They should be willing to put the team before the person and strive together. They lose those insights when we focus on winning at all costs.

Win is a dangerous word. Even if we want all of the positive benefits of sport for our children and strive to teach the real root of competition, using a word like *win* sets off a series of brain processes that may set our kids up like mine—to doubt what's good. I speak for a living on the virtue of sport and the values that matter in life, and yet, my son still thought it was all about winning because that is the word I used most.

I fixed it with my son. You can fix it on your team too.

Instead of asking if they won, ask people how it went. Or say, "Tell me about your game." Open-ended questions that have nothing to do with outcomes are a great way to create analytical and self-evaluative processes in kids. It also reveals what they treasure most about the sport and the game.

Set goals for the team that have less to do with outcomes and more to do about tasks, processes, and mastery. If the goals and focus are on the processes, then the players see what is valued more and get more excited about those things.

Celebrate wins with perspective. There's always more to learn. Couch wins in what it did to help them learn. Point out the process and mastery wins, even without a scoreboard win, to keep them focused on *why* they won. If they know they won because of good values, playing well, and excelling at things they worked on in practice, that will matter more in the long term.

Celebrate the learning that happens in the losses. Don't show too much disappointment with a loss. It is okay to not be satisfied. It is not okay to "lose it" over a loss. Think of losses as those events that reveal the things you can work to improve. It highlights where strengths may be and how to bolster those areas that need work. There is also a character-based victory in every loss, a lesson or value that can be learned and applied in the future. Growth happens in those moments.

The goal is to shift the narrative from "win at all costs" to "compete at all times."

Do as the New Zealand All Blacks and "sweep the shed." Win or lose, they clean up their locker room after every game because "only an All Black should clean up after an All Black." They did a job and they need to make sure they clean up after the job. It humbles them in victory and resets their minds in defeat.

I want your teams to win because it is part of the game. I don't want your teams to be solely focused on winning. They should hear that word less than the process, mastery, and task words. They should hear words that focus them on behaviors and choices, that keep them wanting to work hard, or that help them master the skills they want to learn. If you stop using *win* with your players, you will experience a much bigger win.

Chapter 17

|

Shifting the locus of control back to our team gives them
confidence, resilience, power, and passion for the process.

"Because I said so."

That was my response when my son asked why he had to go to
soccer practice that night. The response was more a knee-jerk reaction
than something I thoughtfully considered. Had I thought it through, I
would not have said it.

I loathed those words growing up. I knew I had no control of
the situation the moment my parents invoked the "because I said so"
amendment. All conversation ceased; there would be no counter, and I
knew I had no say in the matter.

My son was struggling with soccer. He moved clubs mid-season—
by my doing. I had transferred to become the executive director at a

new club over the winter break but left our boys at my old club. The thought was that it would be easier to make the change during tryouts so it would not disrupt their friendships and cause less hardship for the club. I was doing it as a gesture of respect and ethics.

I made few friends within the administration of my old club. This was mainly because I spent the better part of three years trying to change a toxic culture. I was the squeaky wheel who spoke out when coaches were verbally abusive or treating players like numbers and not humans. I was the "voice of discord" when parents were treated as a cancer and often tried to reason with my colleagues to change our MO. I pointed out all the times I believed ethical lines were blurred.

I always used science, logic, and proven methodology to prove my point, but I was *that guy*. Because I was that guy, I had my share of enemies among the Jockacracy, and when I finally had enough, I had several in-depth conversations with the Board president, sent my fifteen-bullet-point letter, outlining all of the reasons I could no longer be a part of what was happening, and jumped ship to a club that gave me *carte blanche* to run it my way (honestly, the proven way to succeed).

I naively thought my kids and their teammates should not shoulder this burden, and, since they were kids, things would work out fine. That was dumb. They became targets for the vitriol. At first, it was passive-aggressive, but then I heard that a director at my former club publicly state he was going to make their experience miserable to get back at me. This is the same director I harangued for calling a group of nine-year-olds "donkeys," so I was fairly certain that person would deliver on his promise to punish me through my boys.

So I pulled them. They had no say in the matter. They did not get to choose whether I moved clubs, and they had no say in whether I pulled them mid-season. It was my call, but the ramifications were their consequences to bear. My decisions were affecting their sports experience.

So there I was. My son was sitting in the back seat of the van, crying. He didn't know anyone on his new team. He didn't feel any confidence on the field. He missed his friends. And he didn't understand why he had no say in any of it. In retaliation, he refused to go to practice and sat in the van, angry tears directed at me.

He was angry because his locus of control was completely external. There was nothing he could be in charge of related to this situation. Mid-season meant he got whatever number was available. I am fairly certain #43 would not have been his first or even fifty-first choice. He had to be put on whatever team had a vacant spot. It wasn't a bad team, but it wasn't *his* team—the one he had known for three years. The team with whom he had forged strong bonds, learned from, and matured with—where he had connected. I know he would not have left his coaches. He loved his coaches. In fact, I was one of his coaches, which made this all the more difficult for him because I was not coaching him or anyone.

With four simple words, I withdrew all remaining threads of control from my son and hijacked his youth sports experience. I proved to him this was not about him at all, but about me. His experience, his learning, his fun—it was mine to control and direct as I pleased. I would venture to guess he "hated" me to some minor degree at that point.

This is what *I* has the danger of doing in a performance realm. My example is certainly extreme, but it is revealing about the shift of control that can happen when we refuse to allow our charges to have power in the process. Power is simply influence. Influence is never neutral. It is negative, positive, or absent. Absent is sometimes worse than negative, and in this case, I had left my son with absolutely no influence over the situation.

"Then I quit. It's your stupid game, and I no longer want to play it!" He screamed at the top of his lungs.

My son knows I am a word person. He knows words have this immense power to break brains within milliseconds. He broke my brain, my heart, and my soul in a flash. I realized then the terrifying peril of *I* when used in the wrong way. He was quitting because he no longer had any influence over what was supposed to be his childhood sports experience. I had mine. He knew that.

His words were powerful and prescient. "It's your stupid game" told me he saw himself as simply a passenger on this ride. A ride that was meant for him had turned into a ride I used to suck out my own needs and wants, with him as the pawn.

I Shifts the Locus of Control

Shifting control is what we do as leaders when our language is centered on us. We do this when we tell our players, "I want you to do this." We don't let them explore the game and develop their own solutions; we tell them what we want as coaches. It's our way or the highway.

We shift the locus of control when we tell our employees, "I am happy with this result." This seems like a compliment or praise, but in reality, it reaffirms that they carried out *our* orders, and we're taking the credit.

I have seen this play out on podiums at youth tournaments. I was at a high-level competition, and one of our teams won. It was a nail-biting, hard-fought couple of weeks of games to get the cup, and the group had worked hard all season to get there.

At the podium, the person in charge of the entire club, who had never once worked with the team, took the microphone and talked for several minutes about how much effort he had put into building this team and moving the club toward success. He talked about his role in how they did and how proud he was to be the leader of such a fine group.

The looks on the faces of the players told a different story. They were teenagers. They knew the effort *they* had put in and the absence of effort on his part. They looked puzzled; some looked crestfallen that their moment of success had been hijacked. He even jumped in the picture to hold the Cup with the team. Photo-op granted.

I was sure I had misread the situation, so I sidled up to one of the players and offered congratulations. I told him, "Huge congratulations. You worked hard for this and earned it. You must be proud of yourself and your teammates." My words were taken directly from research by people such as Carol Dweck. I put all of the control back in the player's court. His response was a moment of clarity for me regarding how we leaders can take away the credit at a moment's notice (and hopefully learn better and give it back).

"Yeah, we busted our [tails]. I don't even know who that guy is, but he had nothing to do with us and now he wants to hold the cup."

Need I say more about using the word *I*. Telling our students, employees, or teams how hard we worked to get them where they are—or even simply how proud we are of them—shifts the locus of control. We psychologically sabotage all of the internal drive it took to get them there. We steal their moment of glory.

How many times had I said "I" during award ceremonies and silently undermined the real work? How many times did I jump in front of the local journalist to give the low-down on the game and remove the players from the equation? I once watched an interview of a professional coach where he stepped aside and said to the reporter, "Why don't you ask the people who were on the field?" A brilliant redirect to those who matter most in the equation: the actors. We can take all the credit we want for the work our teams do, but in the end, all we do is take their control, burn them out, and leave them disconnected. They won't feel any influence over the situation, and they will feel, sometimes not even knowing why, a lack of trust toward us as their leaders.

No one gets to the top of Everest alone.

Educators know, better than most of us, the power of leaving *I* out of the vocabulary during performance-based communication. They continually reinforce the learner, place praise on the effort and strategy the learner used, and help the learner develop their own solutions.

They avoid telling students, "I want you to do it this way" and, instead, try to use phrases like, "Another method *you* could use is . . ." When a student succeeds, teachers don't say things like, "I knew you could do it." Instead, they say, "You must be proud; you discovered the solution."

Educators also know the value of using questions to get learners to focus on the process, help them own their development, and be empowered to take risks. This goes so much further back than formalized education. This goes back to Socrates himself. The Socratic method is about questioning students to get them to think. To reveal their didactic process and understand the many pathways to an answer. He questioned them so they owned the solutions and the outcomes. Today, educators do not say, "I have the answer; let me do it for you." They ask questions to get students to seek and find the solutions themselves.

In performance-based environments, we can continue to eradicate the peril word *I* and inject more *you*s and more questions. Be willing to allow your students to try and also fail, to find solutions, to have influence over the process, and to get all the credit when they succeed. Shifting the locus of control back to our team gives them confidence, resilience, power, and passion for the process.

It is not easy to eliminate *I*. Even those of us well aware of the word's impact struggle with it slipping into our communication daily, but being intentional is a vital piece of the solution. In addition, here are a few simple changes you can make to help your teams become more analytical and independent.

1. Let them have all of the credit. Shift how you praise and how you accept success. Instead of using *I*, shift your language to say

"you" when they win and "we" when they lose. Acknowledge their role in any success and your role in not fully preparing them during failure. Then, they see you as a vital team member, but they see the influence they have over the entire process. Better yet, let them have the limelight. It took a long time for me to realize that those who really matter know the role a leader, coach, or teacher plays in it. Our team members know the role we play, and they are the only ones that matter.

2. Remove *I* when teaching new skills or offering solutions. Instead, tell them things like "a good method for you to use in this situation is . . ." It is a small change from "I would do it this way," but it creates a monumental shift in the relationship and influence.

3. Finally, ask more questions. Instead of immediate answers, make queries that allow them to self-evaluate and find the wins and losses in the situation. Even at the youngest ages, humans are very astute at getting to the bottom of what went wrong and identifying solutions. Watch a baby learn to walk, and you can see how good we are at finding solutions when allowed to have that control.

The brilliance of the Socratic method is that he and his colleagues didn't simply promote their knowledge; they transferred it to others and then allowed those others to develop new knowledge. Without this questioning framework, entire bodies of knowledge would have died with the original thinker, and new bodies would not have developed. Instead, we see the Socratic method as responsible for the foundation of all of academia. We transfer knowledge and grow more because we were willing to shift the locus of control regarding learning over to those doing the learning.

Now that you know the secret, I want you to say *I* a lot less to your teams. (See what happened there?)

Chapter 18

CAN'T

———◆———

Just as we shouldn't give our athletes and team members all of the answers, we should also be willing to let go of limiting beliefs and not give them all of the barriers.

Do you know Iron Man? The iconic and eccentric genius who has powers, even awesome one-liners, and saves the world? You know? Tony Stark?

Would you ever tell the fictional Tony Stark, "You can't do that"?

Of course not. You don't bet against a Marvel superhero genius like that. You nod approvingly, hope he doesn't cause too much chaos, and wait for him to do what others think can't be done—like save his own life with a small device embedded in his chest, build flying suits, create a way to transfer money without actually transferring money, develop fully electric cars, and launch rockets into space for "civilian" interstellar travel.

Okay, those last three weren't done by Tony Stark. They were done by another man, whom many believe was the prototype for Tony. In fact, John Favreau is rumored to have sent Robert Downey Jr. to spend time with this guy to prepare for his *Iron Man* role.

I am talking about Elon Musk. The real-life Iron Man. The guy who was told he couldn't do something so many times, it became white noise in his ears while he was doing it.

Elon was told, "You can't make money off of business advertising on the internet"—which was called silly and wasteful at the time—but he sold his first company Zip2 for over $307 million in 1999. He was only twenty-seven.

Then Elon was told, "You can't transfer money digitally between people. You need a bank and cold hard cash to do that." I guess he was wrong when he bet the farm on PayPal?

No. No. He sold that company for $1.5 billion to eBay in 2002. Elon Musk was used to being told things can't be done, so he didn't flinch when his SpaceX, Tesla, and Hyperloop ideas received the old "mm-hmm, sure" treatment.

In 2017, Tesla was becoming a genuine threat in the auto industry and was the first automobile startup since Chrysler in 1925. That is some seriously elite company. It has a market cap of $30 billion.

SpaceX has now launched NASA rockets successfully twenty-two times (to date) and is groundbreaking in solving the space travel concept.

Hyperloop is in its infancy but showing great promise, just like the other companies he built on the back of the word *can't*. What many saw as impossible, Musk saw as opportunity. He is compared to Henry Ford in the auto industry, Howard Hughes in the aviation realm, and Steve Jobs in terms of innovation. For a man told, "You can't" as many times as he has, he sure seems to be doing a whole lot.

Can't Creates a Fixed Mindset

This is the peril of *can't:* it creates a fixed mindset for most people. The lucky ones who believe anything can be done if you study, work hard, take risks, and remain diligent end up doing what most of us can't. They have a growth mindset, but mindsets can easily shift based on talk. Whether it is the words of someone else or our self-talk, words can limit our beliefs and, thus, our behaviors.

Can't is one of those words that prevents us from seeing the fully possible future. It provides most with a tidy and simple cop-out. Why try, when others say it can't be done?

When our team members hear the word *can't,* it gives them an excuse to move on to other options, take a break, or quit altogether. *Can't* is the large rock covering the entrance to a cave of jewels. It is the forbidden jungle between us and the Promised Land, and it is much easier to see the *can't* and decide it wasn't meant to be rather than say, "I'll show you."

Can't is a word for those without vision or a belief of those too afraid to risk. It should not be a word used with our teams if we expect to create the highest performance possible. *Can't* is a handbrake when an accelerator may be what's needed. It takes less courage to say *can't* than to say, "Why not?"

"Why not?" was one of my favorite phrases growing up. My father was a big motivation guy. My earliest memories are of reading Zig Ziglar's quotes and the biographies of famous people overcoming all odds. When I was barely a teen, my dad gave me a book called *The Edge.* A wrestling coach wrote it, and it contained stories and quotes of people succeeding in the face of unbelievable odds. I wish I still had my copy. It was a library of *why nots* from which I drew great inspiration during my sporting days.

Roger Bannister knew "you can't break the four-minute mile," but he couldn't hear the naysayers over the sound of his feet pounding the pavement to the fastest mile on earth. Fred Astaire was labeled as someone who "can't sing . . . can't act," but he was too busy lighting up the silver screen to realize he shouldn't be there. Wilma Rudolph's polio was so bad, she was told she would be lucky to walk. I guess she was too busy running into Olympic fame to worry about the doctor's fixed mindset.

Our teammates need more *why nots* and less *can'ts* if we want to see them reach their peaks. A word like *can't* sets off a series of processes that limit our ability to perform. We hear *can't* and our brain stops aspiring. It believes we have reached a dead-end, and therefore, we must either stop, turn back, or seek a different route. It can shut down flow, reduce risk, and lower self-efficacy. Our brain wants harmony between what we believe and what the world tells us. If we are not in harmony with the world around us, our brain tends to take the easy path and succumb to the will of those leading us. Instead of believing we can, we simply accept we can't and the dream dies.

This is true unless your team is comprised of the rare people who simply won't accept *can't*. Though there are enough of these stories to fill a library, there are far more of us "average Joes" who fixed our minds on the fact we were not born to do whatever it was we were told couldn't be done. If we all had a strong enough "warrior brain" to excel beyond *can't*, those stories wouldn't be as interesting or inspiring to read. We consume them because those individuals did what we wish we could. They asked, "Why not?"

> **The thing that frustrates me most about "can't" is in the few seconds it took to explain why you can't do something, you could have taken a shot. And worse, someone else did. They are much closer to can now.**

Take some time to research and share with your team the stories of Elon Musk, Albert Einstein, Thomas Edison, Oprah Winfrey, Steve Jobs (fired from his own company!), and so on. They provide the backdrop for getting your team members to understand that *can't* is a dangerous word when it holds no relevance.

This isn't about overconfidence or false beliefs. There are times when deterring someone from injury or a path that is not healthy or conducive to the greater good makes sense, but saying *can't* because no one has yet to do it is silly. Be fair and patient in adhering to standards and rules to ensure safety and mission focus. Stop people when it is well worth it, but do not use the fact it hasn't been done as the excuse for shutting down a dream.

Instead, you can teach your team to strategize when the rock is in the mouth of the cave. Instead of *can't,* use the phrase, "Why not?" When faced with a daunting task and morale seems low, ask them why they could do it. Why not try it and see what happens? You can always soften the ego blow of failure with the whimsical belief, "What's the worst that can happen?" Though not a strong statement, it moves people off of the blockage and onto a risk belief.

When *can't* pops up in a team member conversation, shift the perspective. We have already addressed the concept of *yet.* Be willing to surrogate confidence to your team members by reminding them that just because they can't do it now, it does not mean they can't do it soon. *Yet* is a great method for developing a growth mindset in place of the fixed mindset.

Be willing to ask more questions instead of providing barriers. Just as we shouldn't give our athletes and team members all of the answers, we should also be willing to let go of limiting beliefs and not give them all of the barriers. As leaders, we gravitate toward dictating instead of guiding. We bark out solutions to problems they could solve on their own, and we call out dogmatic limits to their work when we fear they will fail. It's not our role to push and pull them to and from solutions and failures. It is our role to help them develop and grow so they are autonomous, analytical, and empowered to succeed. To do this, we need to be willing to ask questions, even if we believe there is a *can't* in there.

Walt Disney was told he was not creative in his first job. Thank goodness he refused to listen to the expert leaders around him. When a team member wants to try something, just ask questions. Find out why, what, when, and how and let them decide if it is worth doing or not.

This idea of letting team members try their own paths is what helps cultivate mastery and excellence in people. It gives them the ability to build their self-efficacy and create their own skills. "Failure is not fatal; failing to change is." (John Wooden), and preventing teammates from taking those risks is akin to failure as leaders.

Why not be the leader who lets go and lets team members manage the process? You might be surprised by the level of performance achieved when they all develop confidence, growth mindsets, and determined spirits. If you want to see peak performance, you can't keep saying *can't*.

Chapter 19

I KNOW

There is something shortsighted and wholly unacceptable about refusing to listen to fresh evidence.

It was the mid-1900s. In the maternity clinic of the Vienna General Hospital, an assistant to the professor was perplexed by the alarming number of women dying during childbirth because of puerperal, also known as childbed fever.

After studying giving birth on the back versus giving birth on the side and the presence of a priest ringing a bell as possible factors in the high incidence of deaths, the assistant turned his attention to the one difference between doctor-led childbirths and midwife-led childbirths—autopsies.

The midwives had lower death rates than the doctors. The one constant that appeared in all of the cases was that the doctors were performing autopsies after deaths while the midwives weren't. In a panic to find a cure, doctors immediately rushed to the morgue to study the bodies of their deceased patients.

The assistant, Ignaz Semmelweis, surmised the link to the deaths was related to the fact the doctors were potentially carrying some particles of the deceased back to the maternity clinic and transferring the germs to the living. His wild theory was further strengthened by the fact a physician who cut his finger during an autopsy died of the same disease as the women. Until then, it was believed the disease was only contracted by pregnant women.

Emboldened by this additional evidence, Semmelweis studied the best methods for removing particles of the deceased after autopsy. He chose chlorine to remove the odor, not realizing it was a powerful eradicator of germs, and lo-and-behold, the death rates began to fall in the cases where doctors . . . wait for it . . . washed their hands.

Semmelweis was not known as a man of tact, and he demanded that all doctors wash their hands with chlorine before assisting with childbirth. He became so convinced of his theory, he publicly berated those who would not acquiesce to his "request." Doctors fought against him. They openly ridiculed and harassed Semmelweis until he was ultimately fired from his role at the hospital amid public embarrassment.

Thousands of lives could have been saved if only doctors would have listened to him. Instead, Semmelweis became so enraged at the reaction to his theory that he wrote letter upon letter to prominent European obstetricians, urging them to wash their hands. He was so angry that some of his letters would call the doctors who didn't wash their hands irresponsible murders. This anger and obsession led many of his colleagues, and even his wife, to deduce he was losing his mind. In 1865, he was committed to an asylum under suspicion that he had gone insane.

He died only fourteen days after being committed—from an infection similar to the one he had fought to cure. Talk about an ironic twist of fate! Semmelweis was redeemed years later, after Louis Pasteur's germ theory proved he was correct. A sad consolation is Semmelweis is today seen as a pioneer in antiseptic procedures in medicine.

We now know that handwashing is one of the single most important activities in any medical domain, and yet, it was seen as so preposterous that very few doctors believed Semmelweis's pleas for it.

Can you imagine the response of doctors when Semmelweis, a mere assistant to a professor, accosted the doctors?

"I am a highly trained professional. I know what I am doing!"

The Semmelweis Reflex is a metaphor for the instinctive reaction we have when new knowledge is contradictory to established knowledge, norms, or practices.

In high-performance or specialized-skill domains, the Semmelweis Reflex is all too common. Present a top performer who has mastered the skill and tactics with new, contradictory knowledge, and you will most likely get a backlash response . . . or a simple, "I know."

I Know Stalls Development

I know are two of the most dangerous words in our language. They thwart the advancement of practices, methods, and knowledge. They shut down the evolution of a domain. They also cause a breakdown in relationships within teams.

No one, especially experts in their fields, likes to be told they are wrong. They definitely do not want to know that their methods might be hurting others. Can you picture doctors (who swore on the Hippocratic Oath) being told they are killing their patients?

This would create a bad case of cognitive dissonance—when what we believe about ourselves is contradicted by outside evidence. We all want to believe we are good and that we do good in the world. Coaches, doctors, and teachers—all vow to transform lives and cannot fathom when the transformations they create become negative.

Athletes, students, and high-performing employees all have a goal of success and being of value to the world around them (or at least to their team or teachers). They would likely lash back at contradictory evidence.

I know is the backlash. It's that Semmelweis Reflex from someone seeking to do good and be good when they are told they are doing something wrong. It is a gut reaction that erupts when they are given new knowledge that contradicts their current body of knowledge and action.

I see this nearly every time I speak in a room of coaches or experts who still believe the "old-school" way of coaching gets results and breeds success. The "old-school" way hasn't changed in fifty years, yet medicine changes nearly every year.

We could not possibly fathom today's surgeons using leeches to cure a disease or flying across the country on an airplane made just like the Wright Brothers' first one. We wouldn't dare fight a five-alarm blaze using a 1900s fire truck, but we'll still coach kids the same way it's always been done.

There is something shortsighted and wholly unacceptable about refusing to listen to fresh evidence. It seems terribly narrow-minded not to embrace a simple task, such as washing hands, to save lives.

> **Typically, the one thing we learn after saying, "I know" is that we didn't know.**

I know hurtles us back to 1847, standing in the maternity clinic with Ignaz Semmelweis, closing our minds to the opportunity to grow. *I know* severs the tie between leaders and those being led and threatens the development process in the learning environment.

It should be a phrase approached with trepidation. Honestly, it should be a phrase removed from any performance environment anywhere. I picture the sullen teenager, knowing no parent could have possibly learned when he or she was in school, scornfully dismissing that parent at the first sign of showing wisdom. "I know!" scoffs the teen, ridiculing the obtuse adult. What wisdom could the adult possibly have to offer? What a shame those being led aren't willing to learn to lead. What a shame leaders aren't willing to also be led. *I know* keeps both from developing into better versions of themselves.

Team members who say "I know" to teammates or leaders are closing off avenues of growth and reducing the ties that bind them as a team. *I know* can affect the relationships of our teammates. It gives off an air of a "know-it-all" and changes others' opinions of us. It also tells others that someone is not willing to listen. This can severely hinder team continuity and unity.

There are simple methods for combatting *I know*, for both the recipient and the user of the phrase. Instead of declaring new knowledge, try offering it as a suggestion, such as, "What if" or "How about . . ." We avoid attacking the egos of the recipients. This may seem trivial, but imagine how much easier it is to lead and educate people who are not on the defensive. Once the ego is allayed, people are much more open to hearing alternate suggestions.

When offering new information, try to offer it as an option instead of an order, at first. The more skilled or elite a person becomes, the less they like and respond to orders. There are circumstances and certain professions that provide a framework where orders are necessary and accepted, but in most settings, we need to create situations of empowerment in those we lead. If you have knowledge that can help people succeed, frame it as an option first. If they are asked to try something new, they will resist less than if they are ordered to do it.

For instance, suggesting a new way to cook a steak to a very successful chef rarely goes well (no pun intended). I did this recently. At first, he was not amenable to hearing a better way of preparing steak, considering steak was one of his specialties, but I phrased it as an option. I asked if he had ever tasted the "reverse sear," explained what it was and the result of it from my steak-eating experience, and then offered it as an option if he wanted to try something crazy. He relented and loved it. Had I ordered him to do it, I doubt he would have been as interested in learning it.

Finally, when presenting new knowledge, frame it in a way whereby the learner has to discover it for themself. I once had a mentor in the consulting world tell me that every great idea I had would only be great if I could convince my clients it was their idea. In other words, when someone "comes to a new idea or knowledge" on his own, they tend to adopt it and recall it more easily. This is the strength of guided discovery in classrooms. Teachers want learners to gain knowledge by discovering it themselves. The teacher guides the process but allows for this "revelation" to take place organically with the learner. As a consultant—and as a coach—this meant setting up the environment so the learners would discover what it was I wanted to teach, but they had to come to it all on their own.

A few bonuses from guided discovery are the learners own it more, remember it longer, and use it more often after discovering it themselves.

Transformational Words— Words that Transform People and Moments

Chapter 20

C.A.N.T.

There is something almost primal that is triggered
in us when we are challenged.

We were standing at the edge of the ocean. It was a typical Southern California day with bright blue skies and not a cloud in sight. My family and I were following our routine of spending Saturday afternoon at the beach.

The kids were out in the surf with their body boards, riding the small swells up to shore. My wife ventured into the water with them and borrowed a board. She turned to me with that huge smile she always wears at the beach.

"Come on. Ride some waves with me!" She called over the pounding of the surf onto the sand. I waved from my ankle-deep spot on the beach. The water was cold. My feet were plenty deep.

My youngest son urged me to join them. I waved off the invitation with excuses of cold water, horrible tan lines, and a long week.

"I'm good. I'll watch from here and then take a nap on the blanket for a bit."

My other two children joined in the harassment. They were making chicken sounds and playing the "this is our family time" card. I wasn't budging. The water was frigid. I was concerned about having back spasms because of the cold or twisting the wrong way. Plus, I really could use a tan and a few weeks at the gym before taking off my shirt at the beach!

"Seriously, honey. This is such a blast. You need to come in and try it," my wife pleaded.

"I can't."

"Hey! Challenge accepted, no take-backs!" My youngest yelled, and with that, I was trapped by my words.

The rest of the day was a blur of bliss and joy. Riding wave after wave on the body boards, running into the cold surf, and even playing a little beach football, capped by a lot of laughter.

In our household *can't* means, "Challenge accepted, no take-backs." Several years back, when my son was complaining about not being able to complete a math assignment, I had come up with a fool-proof plan to get him to take the risk. In a moment of both frustration and inspiration, I wrote on a piece of paper "C.A.N.T. = Challenge Accepted, No Take-Backs" and handed it to him. I told him *can't* is a word that limits our abilities. It is a cop-out for not trying. It is an excuse to remain still when we could move forward.

"You say you *can't* do the math because you either don't want to, fear failure, or are maybe too afraid to know what happens if you can do it. I think can't simply means you are not willing to." From that moment forward, we decided that anyone who said *can't* was to immediately be challenged to do it and there would be no take-backs.

It has made for some great strides in risk-taking, overcoming fears, and personal growth with our kids and also with us adults in the house. We are a competitive family. No one likes to be challenged, and none of us will back down once C.A.N.T. has been invoked.

It also means we help each other get there. We work together to solve the problem, overcome the obstacle, or complete the task because being the one who challenges also means you are the one who supports.

This acronym has been quite transformative for our family. It has forced us to exit our comfort zones. It has been the impetus for learning new things. It has also been the source of tremendous connection for us. We know if we feel defeated, someone in our family is going to challenge us and refuse to give up on helping us. We know we have support and encouragement at all times.

This philosophy has created confidence in our kids. It has also developed safety and the comfort of knowing we are never alone. We always have someone who will help us overcome the hesitation and who will "cheat lead" us along the way.

It isn't seen as picking on each other when someone states, "Challenged accepted, no take-backs." Instead, it is viewed as a sign of solidarity. As if we are all in this together and want to see each other succeed.

Imagine how powerful C.A.N.T. could be in a team situation. When one individual falters or shows fear, to have teammates immediately leap to support is a very transformational experience. It grows connection, trust, support, selflessness, and empathy. It also means nothing is impossible. A team with a C.A.N.T. culture doesn't see obstacles or failure but opportunities to work together and conquer. They are the teams that eat talent for breakfast because they know they have each other's backs; nothing can stop them, and they have this undeniable spirit to keep going in the face of even the harshest adversities.

There is something almost primal that is triggered in us when we are challenged. We swiftly feel a need to accept the challenge. We do not hesitate to prove ourselves to those who have challenged us. We also do not get discouraged easily in that situation. As a kid, the most dangerous words on the playground are "I dare you" and "no take-backs." These meant social life and death to us. When someone was brazen enough to throw down that gauntlet, it meant our very existence was in jeopardy. If we backed down, we would become a social pariah. If we quit once we started, it would be remembered well through our high school days. There was no escaping the challenge, and there was no stopping once we accepted it.

The ventral tegmental area (VTA) is the area of the brain involved with motivation. It crosses multiple lobes and has a connection to the amygdala. Remember, the amygdala is our lizard brain that tells us to fight or run. Being challenged is motivation. We must choose to stand our ground or flee. This is instinctual and has not changed since our cave days.

The VTA also runs through the frontal lobe, where the self—our analytical abilities—and general executive brain function occur. A challenge that excites the VTA is also a direct challenge to ourselves. We reason that the only option is to accept the challenge and a series of processes are set off to intrinsically motivate us and drive us until the task is complete. Our brain believes our very existence is in danger, and for all intents and purposes, it is. The same section of the prefrontal cortex that lights up when we feel physical pain also alights when we experience social pain, such as the loss of a loved one or the exclusion from a group.

> **Be bold enough to have the courage to fail, the honesty to admit it, and the fortitude to fix it.**[4]

Do you see how being challenged means that section of the brain is on high alert? A failure to accept the challenge could result in exclusion, social humiliation, and social derision. We would rather risk getting our tongue stuck to a frozen flag pole than back down from a challenge.

Now, that is motivational power. That is a transformational process when the brain is both positively motivated by a challenge and negatively motivated by a challenge. This is why C.A.N.T. holds such tremendous power as a transformative word. I highly encourage you to teach your team members to replace *can't* with "Challenge accepted, no take-backs," and here are a few tips to help you do so.

1. Make sure it is stated in an encouraging and supportive way. When my son yelled it out to me over the waves that day at the beach, he was not teasing me or deriding me. He was simply telling me he knew I could do it and wanted to see me take the risk. If it is said in a "bullying" tone, the urge to flee will be much stronger, and individuals will choose the risk of social loss over the fear of further humiliation. It must be stated positively.

2. In addition, be there to support the risk-taker. Once someone has overcome the word *can't*, they need visible support. One of the biggest reasons for taking the risk was someone they trusted indicated a belief in them and intimated they'd be there to assist. Be present and encouraging. Do this a couple of times and *can't* fears disappear quickly in performers. The motivation becomes fully internal, and self-efficacy rises to a level above the fear of failure.

3. Celebrate the wins. No matter how small the C.A.N.T. was, it must be celebrated to enhance its effect. It is only transformative if the person understands its power to help and sees the reward for going through with it. A hundred small victories add up, so no matter the size of the win, if C.A.N.T. is invoked, cheer the win.

4. If there is failure after a C.A.N.T, try invoking *next*. We will not always succeed at everything on the first try, but we fail 100

percent of the times we don't try again. Get the person thinking about the next time they try it. It's okay to miss the mark; it is not okay to quit after that shot.

5. Finally, you must model the behavior. I did not want to get in the water that day. I meant it when I said it was very cold. I was tired. My back was atypically stiff and sore, and as silly as this sounds, I have a confidence issue with taking off my shirt. I have your typical coach's tan lines and no longer feel like the athlete I once was, so I would much rather stay clothed. Yes, it is stupid, but we know how powerful our psychological quirks are. Once my son challenged me, I had to accept it (of course, make sure it is safe, legal, and practical first!). By choosing to accept his challenge, I was showing him the behavior that I hope he displays when he is challenged by the C.A.N.T.

In the end, I had one of my best days at the beach. My confidence has since increased. My family has even more belief in the power of C.A.N.T. In addition, we all believe there is no obstacle too difficult and no challenge we have to face alone. That is a transformative feeling to have for peak performance.

Chapter 21

Help

*The ability to admit when we need help on something
is an inherent and vital learning trait.*

A few weeks after my TEDx Talk went live, I received a private message on Twitter from a very unexpected source. This person is one of the most well-known and well-traveled soccer pundits on the planet.

Their broadcast team covers some of the most high-profile matches in some of the most high-profile leagues. This pundit appears on expert shows, does radio interviews, is a guest on every possible soccer outlet we have, and is considered by many to be one of the best in the business.

Here I am, looking at this private message from a person who I have listened to and watched thousands of times in UEFA, World Cup, CONCACAF, and El Clasico's over the years. I admire this person, look up to this person, and am even slightly envious of this person. To receive a message was unexpected and surreal, but the nature of the message was the biggest surprise of all.

"Would love to chat . . . for some advice . . ." the message read. Advice? From me? In October 2015, I was a youth soccer coach in Cincinnati, Ohio, one who had not traveled the world, had not worked with any coaches, organizations, or governing bodies outside my zip code, and was certainly not sought after for my advice beyond simple coaching tips. To have this expert ask me for help was stupefying.

I voiced that truth when we had our call. I explained how honored I was and how surprised I was to be approached for advice. I wasn't sure if I had much to offer, but I would do my best.

The expert simply said, "I know when to ask for help."

Shouldn't we all be that grounded, that humble, and that vulnerable to admit when we need help? What kind of model would we provide for our children if we set aside machismo and pride to say "help" once in a while?

That moment and that word became transformational for me. I wanted to be an expert and authority on a grand scale and help others by sharing the ins and outs of my learning journey. I had a healthy ego from my years of playing and my coaching successes to that point. I thought I had a gift that the world needed. At that moment, I realized I had so much more to learn, and if I was going to be of any assistance to anyone outside my living room, I better well know when to ask for help myself!

I have been so grateful to that amazing person for the lesson I learned that day. That person continues to be an inspiration, a mentor, and a model of what it means to be an expert, a great human, and a lifelong learner. All because of one word: *help*.

Here is why *help* is such a powerful and transformational word:

Help helps us learn. The ability to admit when we need help on something is an inherent and vital learning trait. Let's go back to a child learning how to walk. That child will work through all the failures, mistakes, and bumps and bruises on their own, but at some point, they will reach out for a little assistance or encouragement. Many times, it is that little bit that catalyzes the learning. Babies know this! They already get how vital asking for help is, and their brains are nowhere near as developed as our adult brains.

This is a common theme in classrooms—asking for help. In fact, an entire learning theory was developed around the concept of *help* in the learning experience. Lev Vygotsky, a Russian education researcher, discovered that children learn best in what he termed the "Zone of Proximal Development." The ZPD refers to that point in learning where someone is challenged enough to avoid boredom, but not so much to hit burnout. Being pressed just out of their level of ability, a learner is in the ZPD and will usually need just a bit of assistance to experience a learning breakthrough. It is that *help,* which the learner seeks, that catalyzes the learning.

The concepts of peer-assisted learning and "scaffolding" are based on this need for *help.* Learners in the ZPD can find success by being paired with a peer who may be slightly more advanced in the topic, and it is that peer who provides the help. Educators who want their learners to be challenged but assisted will scaffold the learning process with this "help" throughout.

Our children learn in school to ask for help when they need it, yet when we place them in performance situations, we make it paramount to never ask for help. We cause them to believe it shows weakness, a lack of skill, or a quitter's attitude. These ideas could not be further from the truth! Asking for help is a sign of a growth-oriented person, a lifelong learner, a person willing to take risks and learn new things. Shouldn't those be the people we want in performance-based scenarios? Further, when people are in situations that call for elite performance, where mistakes can cost a lot more, shouldn't they be encouraged to ask for help to ensure they perform at their very best?

Help is at the heart of learning and is a foundation for performance. It is the kind of word every one of those we lead should know, be comfortable saying, and embrace as vital to success.

It provides safety and security. Not to get too much into the geekiness of psychology, but the concepts of *groupthink* and the *bystander effect* are centered on the idea that, as humans, we are afraid to speak up and go against the grain of the social norm and that we believe our input doesn't matter because someone else will step up in that scenario. This is breaking down the concepts to a basic level, but you can see how important it is for us to never go against the grain and how much we deflect responsibility when others are present.

We will not speak up if we know what we think is not a commonly held belief or action of those around us. Ever been in a meeting, workshop, or lecture and wanted to answer a question or discuss a concept but remained silent? In your head, you likely assumed others might disagree with you, that you might appear stupid to them, or that you didn't want to appear to be "rocking the boat." Rather than raise your hand and speak, you sat idly by and let the moment pass. We all do it.

> **Asking for help is powerful beyond measure. It shows you are wise enough to leverage the strength of others.**

I was in a Tutor Training course for the Gaelic Athletic Association recently and had this exact experience. I have two master's degrees directly related to sports, learning, and coaching. I have thirty years of field experience to back up the research. I know nothing about Gaelic football or hurling, so when the lecturer started asking questions I was certain I knew the answers for, I did nothing! I sat there quietly, stressing that others would think I was stupid if I raised my hand and answered incorrectly. It took me nearly an hour before I finally added my two cents. What is crazy about this is that later, I found out they valued my input dearly because of my unique background and my perspective, which was so different from theirs. They wanted me to speak, and I refused. I did that because I feared the social ramifications of being wrong. More vital in this course were all the questions I had and needed answers to that I had missed out on during that first hour! If only I had been gutsy enough to ask for help. How much more could I have learned and could those in the course have learned alongside me?

Help provides safety, yet we have made it a word that denotes danger. It really is a shame, and my dream would be for that word to be *the* word used in certifications, workshops, and learning environments for those of us that lead and teach others. It brings great security and safety to know we asked for help enough that we got it right when others needed to learn from us.

Going deeper, *help* could save lives. There have been countless situations where one person needed help but didn't speak up because the groupthink was different from their perspectives. In some of those situations, that help would have caught a fatal engineering flaw, a mechanical inconsistency, or a side effect that could have saved lives. Instead, *help* was never uttered.

In a bystander-effect situation, we are convinced that our assistance is of very little significance because someone else more qualified or better equipped will step up to help. Many times, they don't help either. The now famous case of Kitty Genovese serves as a reminder that *help* provides security and safety. She was brutally murdered in the courtyard of a crowded apartment complex with dozens of bystanders who could hear her calls, but no one helped, each one assuming someone else would intervene. No one did. What if we were all empowered to see help as something necessary for the safety and security of us all? That *help* did not mean we were insignificant, but that each of us had the immense power to change the world if we were willing to step out there and be the one who did help. *Help* is a transformative word that should spark a desire in each of us to intervene, support, and be present for those around us.

In a more general way, *help* should be a word all of our charges know instinctively and use regularly. *Help* means I may make a mistake and could use a little guidance. *Help* means I do not feel comfortable with this situation and am worried I could get hurt. *Help* means I am scared and just want some reassurance or a boost to get me there. *Help* means I cannot do this alone, and I need you. I tell my children every chance I get to ask for help unabashedly because it is better to appear a fool for a few moments than to be irreparably hurt for a lifetime, or worse.

Help Models Vulnerability

As I've mentioned before, the New Zealand All Blacks are the greatest and "winningest" sports program in human history. They are also some of the most feared warrior athletes on the planet. They win as a way of life, and they put fear in the hearts of many as part of their pre-game routine. The Haka provides them a distinct advantage, according to former coach Graham Henry, because it is so impressive, powerful, and awe-inspiring. Imagine being an opponent of these massive mountains of muscle and having them scream, chant, and gesture with menacing faces a mere few feet from you before you take the field. I get shivers just thinking about it.

The Haka also calls up the ancestors to go to war with them that day. In other words, when you play the All Blacks, you are not facing off against only fifteen warriors; you are squaring off with a legacy. Over one hundred years of warriors, an ancient culture, a country—a lifetime of tradition—is going to battle against you. It gives them a very distinct boost of confidence and strikes doubt in their opponents' hearts.

They also have a saying: "The best way to get rid of nightmares is to give them to someone else." Think about that phrase for a moment and try not to quiver. Look up a highlight video of the All Blacks and see how menacing, how powerful, how devastating they are. They crush opponents for a living. That is the thing of nightmares.

You may wonder what all this has to do with *help* and the answer is *everything*. For as powerful, confident, menacing, strong, and success-ful as these athletes are, they have a cultural facet as part of their team dynamic that embraces vulnerability. Saying "help" (showing vulnerabil-ity) is a cultural marker, or behavior, that is encouraged and celebrated by the organization and by the country as a whole.

Alongside their strength coaches and Haka creator, they have on-staff psychologists and therapists to assist the players with the everyday pres-sures and accumulating stresses of being elite-level athletes. They know that just as important as the yoga instructor, nutritionist, and physi-cal trainer, the mental therapist is vital to keeping them healthy and safe. Imagine that! A world-class team of warriors, revered for their size, strength, power, and success, employ someone to help them stay men-tally fit too!

The All Blacks are not too "manly" to ask for help when they need it. Whether it is with learning a skill, fixing an injury, or working through some bad mental gunk that has built up inside, they ask for what they need, and they are celebrated for being vulnerable enough to admit it.

Everyone we meet is fighting a battle we cannot see. Few people we meet would ever admit they need help. The fact is, *help* is a word coaches and leaders should model so our players can be taken care of in ways we never even considered. That battle wages on unaddressed until they know it is safe to say, "Coach, I am having a bad month, and I need help. I need someone to talk to about . . ." How much more transformative could we be if we modeled vulnerability to our players so they were tough enough to be vulnerable when they needed us most? We would simply create better athletes or learners—transforming, or even saving, lives.

Use the Word *Help* to Foster Community

Help bonds us with others. It is the kind of word that connects people in a way that goes beyond simple conversations or interactions. When someone asks for help—and we provide it—we connect on a more visceral and ethereal level. We tap into the lizard brain and serve an ancient and instinctual need that exists in all humans.

We are conditioned to connect. Connection meant survival for us when we were hunted by larger and more powerful prey. We unified to hunt more effectively, gather all we needed, and for warmth in the cold weather. Connection is instinctual and when someone is helped, that connection taps right into the Neanderthal brain.

What would it be like to have a team of athletes or employees who were confident enough to say "help"? What kind of connection would develop among those people at a visceral level? How much harder would they work for each other and how much more deeply would they be invested in the team? This is what the word *help* does for teams and people. It bonds them in ways no regular training session can.

Why do you think "team building" is such an effective tool, which corporations spend hundreds of thousands of dollars each year to do? Most team-building sessions have a component that requires participants to work together to solve a problem, to help each other achieve the desired outcome. You could have those kinds of team-building sessions every time you work with your group if they were encouraged to use the word *help*.

Help is an easy transformational word to incorporate into your performance vocabulary immediately. Here are some ways you can begin to use *help* to encourage learning, provide safety, ensure mental fitness, and develop a connection.

1. **Ask for help when you don't know the answer.** You do not have to know all of the answers all of the time. When you don't know an answer, ask your team. Admitting you do not know

something builds trust, makes you more approachable, and teaches your charges to also ask for help when they don't have the answer.

2. **Ask for help when you're having a bad day.** I had a coach who went through a rough patch. It took months, but finally one day, he told us he was having a tough time and asked us to help. We gained so much more respect for him, and we rallied around him. We stayed after practice and just chatted with him. We went to his house one weekend and helped hang drywall and ate pizza. We were present for him. Because of that, he was always present for us. It went way beyond any game or practice relationship; we had formed a deep connection, a bond.

3. **Ask for help with set-up, break-down, and more.** We tell our teams to do a lot for us. Sometimes, reframing the tell into an ask is all it can take to change the outlook of an entire team. People who are asked to help are more likely to provide it happily, to feel empathy with the one asking, and to be more present. Being asked to help set up or break down also engages team members in the process and gives them ownership over everything, not just the training or learning. This is their team, their experience, and their game, and when they play a role in helping with the entire process, they feel that responsibility every step of the way.

Chapter 22

Unlucky

"Unlucky" is a word that can transform outlooks about the game, shift mindsets, and help everyone become more resilient.

I missed the shot. I mean, I didn't just miss the shot; I bombed it two dozen yards wide and at least twenty over the goal. At my old high school, our south end zone sat some thirty yards from the natatorium. I cleared the goal, the fence, and hit the back wall of the natatorium.

I was in the box, all alone, with the ball sitting nicely at my feet, and I sent it for a ride. It was a disastrous effort. Being the kind of athlete who was always in his own head, I immediately launched into a devastating inner dialogue of "what are you doings" and "what the hecks." My brain became a battlefield very quickly.

We were only minutes into the game. This meant it would be a long and difficult night for me. I'd had these nights before many a time.

"Unlucky, Reed!" Coach's voice bellowed across the field. I could hear it clearly above the din of the game.

Unlucky. I'd never heard that word in the context of completely blowing a simple scoring opportunity. I hadn't heard it in the sporting realm at all, but there it was. Completely stopping the imminent mental meltdown.

It became a transformational word. It didn't simply thwart my meltdown; it shifted my mindset completely. Suddenly, I felt calm. I felt almost okay with my mistake. I moved past it and changed how I felt about the shot, the result, and my part in all of it.

It was unlucky. No blame. No missed opportunity. No need to dwell on the *what ifs.* It was just an unfortunate moment in an eighty-minute game filled with both fortunate and unfortunate moments.

How many times had I scored a goal and thought to myself, "Well, that was lucky"? Maybe I was in the right place at the right time or the ball bounced just right. Maybe the keeper just didn't get enough of the ball or the defender deflected it just enough to put it out of reach. When those moments happened, I saw them at face value. I put myself in a position to take advantage of opportunities, and everything worked out in my favor. I worked hard, and I got a little lucky.

So what if that was the case in a mistake? I worked hard, but I got a little unlucky. The ball took a bad bounce at impact, a defender got a piece of my foot as I was striking the ball, or a nearby noise caused me to lift my head. Who knows what happened in those particular moments, but I had to see it at face value. I worked hard but just got a bit unlucky.

My coach was a genius. He'd found a word that could transform my outlook on the game, shift my mindset, and help me become more resilient. That word also helped me transform my perspective on control. I can only control what I can control, and I must let go of that which I cannot control. *Unlucky* allowed me to let go of a lot!

Here's the thing about *unlucky*: Not only is it transformative in the sense it completely changes an athlete's perspective, control, psyche, and more, but it is one heck of a versatile word. It can be applied to so many situations in sports. For me, as a coach, it has become my Swiss Army knife of performance-based communication. It can transform any negative or potentially damaging situation with pithy ease.

Bad referees? When a referee makes a "bad call," *unlucky* tells my players to move on and let go of it. They cannot argue the call, nor should they dwell on it. If I yell at the ref, what does that do for my players? It usually shifts their focus on the ref, too, and then they are stuck in that quagmire of blaming others instead of controlling what they can control. It may also tell the ref that they owe me one without me ever having to say that. It was simply an unlucky call—nothing more. No need to stick on that point.

Embarrassing moments? When a potentially humiliating moment occurs (like a player slips and falls in the open field, we score on our own goal, or the ball goes right through the goalie's hands on a routine squibbed shot), *unlucky* transforms the humiliation into either nothing or humor. Like when agent Maxwell Smart messed up and said, "Missed it by that much." What was damaging becomes humorous. Who hasn't had an embarrassing moment? It's just unlucky.

Unexpected losses? If we lost a game we should have won, *unlucky* is an easy way to brush off the loss and not dwell in the past. Too many times, we want to dwell on something we no longer have control over but that can affect any future performances. The saying goes, "If you spend all your time looking in the rearview mirror, you miss the road ahead." It's one thing to debrief and learn from poor performance, especially when you should have won, but dwelling on it only equates to a lack of progress. Walking away from a bad game, telling my athletes it was *unlucky*, sends a clear sign. "It is over and done, and we are moving on from this." It told them I was not satisfied, but I was not going to get caught up in wallowing in doubt and pity. "Unlucky, grab your gear, spend some time with your family, tomorrow we will make the adjustments we need to make, and I will do better to equip you for success" was a far better conversation than berating my athletes for twenty minutes and running them until they puked. Message received, hit reset, and start again tomorrow.

There are many other situations where *unlucky* applies in performance settings that allow our charges to reset their mental framework and move on from the moment without any lasting negative effects. Many will think you are being flippant at first. I had my share of coaching partners who could not stand the phrase, but they always came around after they saw the Zen-like, freeing effect it had on all of us. It simply released us from the terrible moment.

I'm willing to be unlucky a million times if all it takes is to be lucky once.

As a coach or leader, you can apply *unlucky* in your daily communications as mentioned above or in the following ways:

1. **When you mess up.** Be honest. Have you messed up as a coach? I hope so. I've had far more goofs, gaffs, bloopers, and mistakes in my career than I have had successes, but that is what has made this journey so amazing. When I finally learned to own up to them, give them perspective (like laughing off a demonstration that goes terribly wrong), and drop an "unlucky" label on it, I learned two things. First, it is amazingly cathartic to not have the pressure to always be perfect in front of those you lead or coach. Second, you become a model for how they should handle mistakes and failures. The day I noticed my players laugh-

ing and quipping "unlucky" during a difficult technical training session, I knew they would survive the pressures of youth sport participation and later elite-level performance.

2. **When something doesn't go your way.** Whether it is referees, tournament draws, a media article, the weather, or any other extraneous factor acting as a fly in the ointment, you cannot control it. If you try to control it, you will go crazy. It is much easier to brush it off with an *unlucky* and reframe the things you can control.

3. **When someone is trying a new skill and struggling.** All learners will go through those "desirable difficulties" that happen on the pathway to a mastery of new things. The difficulties can easily lead to frustration and abandonment without that little mental boost. Many times, that boost can be accomplished with a simple *unlucky*. You might say, "Unlucky, you are working so hard and are almost there. Keep going." Then, you have become a road sign that indicates they are heading in the right direction, and the destination is near. They won't abandon the pathway; they will keep going and look for more signs. They won't internalize the failure as something inherently wrong with them, meaning they will never "get it." It is simply an unlucky circumstance. Bonus, if you offer a small tip or adjustment that moves them even further along the path. They still get to solve it themselves, but that little boost may be what they need for a breakthrough.

4. **As a wildcard.** *Unlucky* is one of the most versatile and transformational words in performance-based situations. It applies to many scenarios and all types of learners and creates a plethora of positive outcomes if used correctly and amended with your take on things. Go for it and try *unlucky* where you see fit to help transform someone's mental state when needed. Be sure to share

the times you've found it most helpful . . . that is the magic of words—the ability to share them with others so they, too, can use them with great success.

Chapter 23

Love

A whole slew of good things happen when we lead with love.

Several years back, Coach Mark Richt was with the University of Georgia football program, and one of their biggest games came down to a single field goal. If the kicker made it, they'd win. If he missed, they'd lose and likely miss out on a bowl game.

Bowl games are big money for the schools involved. They are a boost to recruiting as well. In addition, they mean bonuses for the coaching staff and better visibility for NFL prospects. It has a lot of equity attached. Needless to say, this was a "must-make" kick and likely the single most important kick of this young man's career.

The Field Goal Heard 'Round the World

Coach Richt grabs his kicker, pulls him near, and says something into the ear hole of his helmet. The young man trots onto the field, and cool as a cucumber, nails the game-winning field goal. Mission accomplished.

What did Coach Richt say?

At the news conference after the game, that was the question on most reporters' minds. *What did you say?* Coach Richt calmly responded that he told the young man whether he made it or missed it, he loved him.

That is all. No rousing motivational speech about moving mountains, creating legacies, or going down in history. No threats of benching him or revoking his scholarship if he missed. He simply told the young man he loved him as a human instead of only valuing him as an athlete.

The kicker was not some number on a roster. He was not chattel. He was not a mere vehicle to greater wealth or fame for Coach Richt. He was a nervous young man, hoping someone believed in him, and who believed in himself enough to do his job under that intense pressure.

This is how coaching should be. Leading with love. The rest becomes minor details along the journey if an athlete knows they are valued as a person and loved for more than performance.

Leading with love is not a complex strategy, but it is unbelievably hard for many coaches to execute. We have been conditioned to avoid showing emotion, to be detached sages who bestow game-based wisdom and drive our players like oxen to carry out the tasks that bring us greatness.

The media have taught us, along with the tall tales told by our parents, that a coach is hard, terse, and cold. Our job is to toss our athletes into the harsh wilderness like Spartan children and hope the cauldron shapes them into men and women of war.

This is especially true for traditionally masculine sports, like football—the hard nose, helmet slapping, spit-shooting yeller of a coach is the norm. This is the bellicose nature of most sports. Coaches are more like blacksmiths forging iron than artists molding clay. The Mark Richt-like coach is a rare Avis (a rare bird) on the scorched sports landscape.

Mark Richt is more powerful than those hard men. He is more courageous than those Hollywood hate bombs. Coach Richt is more heroic and more needed than those false gods of manhood.

Our athletes need more from us than momentary success in a stressful game. They need connection, a sense of belonging, and a deep-rooted belief that only comes from someone who coaches the person, not just the player. This is not a trite aphorism; it is the truth that "love conquers all." Love is the most powerful emotion we feel as humans and is a tremendous source of strength, courage, and confidence. We are hard-wired to respond to love.

It is an evolutionary phenomenon that saved our lives when we were not quite at the top of the food chain. We connected with others to create safety in numbers, hunt more effectively, and accomplish hard jobs. We survived through connection, and this connection was strengthened by the neurophysiological reaction of love. A feeling of belonging, a feeling of importance and value. By being connected, we felt a special emotion, and when disconnected, we felt pain in the same part of the brain as with physical pain.

Social loss is as hurtful as a physical loss. We feel pain for being excluded or unloved in the same way we would if we lost an arm. This means a "broken heart" might be truly broken. Love is powerful.

It drives a parent to lift a car off or step in front of a train for her child. It drives normally rational human beings to "see red" and commit crimes of passion. It has started wars and destroyed civilization. Love is a powerful influencer, and in sport, it is a keystone that can command an amazingly positive influence.

Imagine what you could accomplish with a team of athletes who would "run through a wall" for you and their teammates. What would that look like? Players so devoted to the cause, loyal to the greater good, and driven by confidence that nothing seemed insurmountable. This would be a force similar to what we see with the vaunted New Zealand All Blacks. Humility, focus, responsibility, loyalty, and love for team, self, and legacy. What a powerful concept.

You'll get all that from telling players you love them. Or more importantly, leading with love. Athletes who know they are loved can accomplish more, play the game longer, and enjoy it much more than those driven by fear. Yet, we see fear-mongering every weekend on the fields of youth sports.

If Mark Richt can show his players how much he cares with his words, why can't the coaches of youth players? We can, but we have to shift our focus. Do we want outcomes, or do we want to transform people?

Mark Richt probably needed that win, but his desire to transform that single young man, and in the process the entire team, compelled him to lead with love. He is focused on people, on process, and on transformation, and his success is just as high as other coaches in his fraternity. We can lead with love and still win? Yup.

A whole slew of good things happen when we lead with love. First off, our players' confidence will spike. Tell someone you love them, and you light that eternal fire of self-belief. Love drives confidence.

Second, leading with love helps athletes trust us, trust themselves, and trust each other. It is a safety net of sorts. A loved athlete feels safe enough to leave the comfort zone, be willing to listen to others, and follow others' advice.

Third, loved athletes are activated. They are fully engaged, empowered, and focused, and this activates every fiber of their being for the cause. They are not simply showing up and "going through the motions"; they are galloping onto the scene and competing fiercely at all times. Loved athletes are all in.

> ## You can demand excellence without
> ## demeaning the person.

Fourth, a loved athlete feels a strong sense of belonging. This sense drives humility, responsibility, discipline, and empathy. When someone feels loved, it creates empathic connections with others. You don't just know what others might feel; you feel it yourself. Love is the great connector of minds and hearts. Even *Friday Night Lights* figured out that a "full heart" can't lose.

Finally, loved athletes are fearlessly happy. They do not fear failure, rejection, or risk. They dive headlong into the learning process because that feeling of connection dispels all fear. And once they dive in, they seek joy. Recall the feeling of euphoria you had when you first fell in love or when you snuggle with your favorite pet. That euphoria is joy. We seek it. In fact, once we taste it, we don't just seek it, we ruthlessly hunt down joy. Ever seen a team that played with such passion and joy-seeking? It is a sight to behold. Lead with love, and your teams will be fearlessly happy.

As I stated earlier, leading with love is not complicated, but it is hard. It is choosing to eschew the false cultural standards of sports and take a risk. It means reframing how you see your athletes and why you coach them, but it is worth it. The reward to a leader who loves is just as magnificent as the reward to the protégé who feels loved. There are a few simple steps you can take to lead with love.

See your players as people who have infinite possibilities beyond the game. They are not there to learn rote skills and collect brass sculptures. They are in sports to be molded, shaped, guided, and compelled to be great people. See them as these excellent people who want to succeed in way more than sports.

Invest personally in your players. Talk to them as people. Spend time with them. Ask them questions and get to know what makes them so unique as people. You leave behind all the world when you step onto the training grounds and focus only on investing in your players. Players who feel invested in, feel loved.

Be very clear about why you do what you do. It cannot simply be about winning, or money, or your ego. It has to be about way more than that for nearly all of us. Very few of us will get rich coaching, like the Nick Sabans of the world. We sacrifice a lot to be out there, and it cannot be for those fleeting mortal wants. Heck, even Nick Saban does it for something other than money. Find your Everest, that mountain you rush headlong to every morning, upon which you would rather spend your waking hours, and then chase it. When you choose to chase your Everest, love will naturally spill out of you.

Tell your players how you feel. Stop being macho, or closed-off, or guarded, and just say it. Tell them how much they mean to you, how happy you are to spend time with them, and how you love them regardless of what they do as athletes. This is the hardest facet of leading with love: saying the word. We have been taught—or learned through trial and error—not to share our love, but that is exactly what youth sports needs. We need more love! So let your players know.

Coaches who lead with love should be the gold standard and not the outlier and until we figure out this fact, we will continue to battle toxicity, attrition rates, and lack of fulfillment in youth sports. Athletes sport to have fun, to belong, to feel safe, and to be loved. Leading with love is simply doing what they want and need. It is not a sign of weakness; it is the most powerful path any human can take, and if you lead with love, they will follow in kind. What a great place youth sports would be if it were filled with love.

Now, as the screenwriters of *Friday Night Lights* crafted, "Clear eyes, full hearts, can't lose." Let's do this.

The Thriver's Prerogative

Chapter 24

A Second Message To Sparta

There comes a time in every person's career when they begin to question their impact on the world.

So the rumor goes, and so I will take my poetic license on this story. There is much less written about this, but some evidence does exist[5] to verify its authenticity.

After Phillip II of Macedonia passed on his chance to conquer Sparta in 346 BC, he had a second chance to win the one trophy that eluded him. Eleven years had passed since Phillip chose not to attack and conquer Sparta. He was turned away by the bold and overreaching imperative to survive shown by the Spartans. A war thwarted by that single, two-letter word, *if*.

Sparta, at the time Phillip sent the emissary, was decimated, decaying, and poor. The land was barren, so Phillip thought nothing of walking away and letting them languish in their small existence. What he took to doing over the next decade was encircling them with others who would join his "league" and keep Sparta in their place. The Spartan enemies were widespread, so the task of getting others, like Argos, to stand with him was quite easy for Phillip.

At this point in his reign, Phillip's son was old enough to become a regent and military advisor, and as it would happen, showed some serious hutzpah as a military leader when he thwarted a city-state rebellion and subsequently named the conquered village "Alexandropoulos." Yes, Phillips's son was none other than Alexander the Great.

In possession of his own "military village" and gaining a more and more competitive spirit, Alexander was now no slouch on the battlefield, and though he may not have realized his son would go down as one of the greatest military leaders in history, Phillip had to have had an inkling of his son's prowess.

There comes a time in every person's career when they begin to question their impact on the world. The "what have I done" self-talk was strong in Phillip. He had extended his empire and expanded his wealth, and yet, one life-defining feat had eluded his grasp. With his son gaining momentum like a juggernaut, one has to wonder if Phillip wanted one last chance to impress the young Alexander and show him "Dad still has it." Phillip fixed his gaze squarely on Sparta once more.

He showed the same respect for the fierce and mighty warrior state that he had the first time and sent a second note to them. He had learned from his first failed attempt. His note gave them no option. No chance to turn his words around on him. He would not be vague or filled with doubt or allow for an alternate interpretation. He would be as laconic as they were.

His note was simple, powerful, direct, and undeniable. There was no doubt of his next move. He prepared his note and sent it along. Then he waited for the reply.

His note read, "I will enter your land as either friend or foe."

Just as the Spartans had years before, they made him wait. And just as the Spartans had when all they had was the need to survive and keep the once-great state relevant, they answered him in one simple word.

How could the Spartans interpret his note in any other way than a veiled threat to conquer them? Phillip had a foothold in all the lands surrounding Sparta, the loyalty of all the other city-states, the anger of Sparta's enemies, and the momentum of his son behind him. There was nothing to debate. Phillip had the Spartans dead to rights on this one. Their best move was to befriend him, bow to him, and join his growing league of Hellenic city-states as a pseudo ally.

> **Use the language of excellence long enough and you not only survive, you begin to thrive.**

But . . . these are the Spartans we are referring to, and they were born to fight. They were raised to be uncomfortable. They were trained to die on the battlefield, for only a Spartan who dies in battle gets a gravestone! Phillip was clear and concise, he left no room for doubt, and yet the Spartans found a way. They found a way to assert their dominance, via language, and show their power with another single word.

Their response: "Neither."

Conclusion

The Prerogative to Thrive

*Thriving is about process over product,
values over victories, and spirit over sport.*

Words hold great power over mankind. They build up, tear down, reset things, and set off firestorms in our brains and on the battlefields of life and sport. For the Spartans, *if* was a survival mechanism. It gave them one more breath. One more chance to stay alive. One last, gasping day in the sun. As we now know, *if* gave them eleven years.

That imperative to survive stalled the inevitable for eleven additional years. It was plenty of time for them to rebuild, replenish, and rearm for the battles life would throw at them. They did just that too. They shifted from surviving to thriving in those eleven years and shifted their mindsets from one of "last gasps" to "breaths of freedom." Once you've taken the journey and grown along the way, you no longer feel compelled to merely survive. You are emboldened with confidence, power, and the grit to thrive.

Recall our skateboarder who fell thirty-four times in his quest to master that elusive trick. Each fall was greeted with more determination and a need to survive the journey. Each time he dropped in to try the trick again, he knew he was one moment closer to mastery. He was one step closer to the summit of his Everest.

When he succeeded at the trick, an amazing thing happened. He did not plant a flag on that mountain and retire. Not a chance. It became the first of many ticks. That was merely another stepping stone on the bigger journey for him, but he had fully ingrained the Excellence Ethos so he could face down any adversity, stand tall against any foe, and move forward against all defeats because he knew, first and foremost, he could survive.

The Excellence Ethos is about cherishing the challenges we face, knowing we are being shaped into something greater by them. It is about mastering all we do, knowing that mastery leads to long-term success and joy. It is about honing in on the beauty of the relentless pursuit of being a better person today than you were yesterday because that is what will help you succeed in the greater game of life.

Finally, it is about process over product, values over victories, and spirit over sport. Those seeking everyday excellence don't play to win; they transcend the game itself to shift from surviving the game to thriving in life. That trumps any win.

We write the code that takes us beyond "getting by," beyond wins and losses, and beyond momentary successes. We write code that teaches us to thrive.

That is the most important takeaway from this book. There are words we use that can help guide our greatest performances in sport. Some words lead to peril and keep us trapped in the game itself, a victim of our mental malware. Others are power words that give us a fighting chance to survive, just as the word *if* did for Sparta. They are the code that transforms things.

And once we learn to harness the power of words—the codes—and survive, we begin to realize what motivates and accelerates the brain, and we discover that we stop merely surviving. We write the code that takes us beyond "getting by," beyond wins and losses, and beyond momentary successes. We write code that teaches us to thrive. Where no challenge is too insurmountable, no foe is too scary, and no loss too final to recover. We are not defined by those words but driven by them. This code gives us the ability to thrive in every moment of our competitive lives and beyond. It empowers us to invoke the Thriver's Prerogative.

To prosper, grow well, and flourish in sport, in class, in work, and, most importantly, in life, because that is the right and privilege of every person in this world. And now, you have the tools to do so.

Go do it. Your journey is not complete, and you will thrive the next time you face a challenge. I believe in you.

About the Author

Leveraging two master's degrees—in sports psychology and early childhood development—and thirty years of professional coaching experience, "Coach Reed" Maltbie has dedicated his life to creating the best environments for athletes of all ages to achieve peak performance, on and off the sports field. Coach Reed has implemented training programs with all types of sports organizations—Gaelic  Games Association, US Sailing, USA Hockey, USA Swimming, Ontario Volleyball, US Olympic and Paralympic Committee, Soccer Canada, and PGA of Canada, to name a few. As a former Division I athlete, Coach Reed is no stranger to the impact of language in eliciting peak performance. He shared his own experience with the power of words in his 2015 TEDx Talk, "Echoes Beyond the Game," and has contributed educational content to hundreds of media outlets, such as *The Huffington Post*, NBC Sports Engine, ESPN Radio, and Sirius XM FC shows, "Coaching Academy" and "Beyond the Pitch." A seasoned public speaker and motivator, Reed has also published multiple coaching resources, including a chapter in the textbook, *Youth Sports in America*, and the coaching program and tool cards, *Positive Discipline Tools for*

Coaches, which was released in three languages. The essential work he has done through keynotes, workshops, webinars, and courses in the sports space has supported hundreds of thousands of athletes and tens of thousands of coaches on five continents. Today, he resides in San Diego, California, with his wife and three kids, where he continues to serve the sports community while developing programs that help everyday competitors unlock peak performance in their respective fields through his new venture: Everyday Excellence.

Endnotes

1   Snyder, Zack, dir. *300*. Montreal: Icestorm Studios, 2006, Nationwide release.

2   *Friday Night Lights*, Season 1, Episode 1. "Pilot." Directed by Peter Berg. Aired October 3, 2006 on NBC. Now streaming on Peacock, https://www.peacocktv.com?cid=20200101evergreenownyt002&utm_source=youtube&utm_medium=owned_onlinevideo_brandawareness_descriptionlink.

3   John F. Kennedy Presidential Library and Museum, speech at Rice University, 12 September 1962, public domain, accessed July 21, 2022, https://www.jfklibrary.org/learn/about-jfk/historic-speeches/address-at-rice-university-on-the-nations-space-effort.

4   Coach Reed Maltbie, "Echoes Beyond the Game: The Lasting Power of a Coach's Words," filmed July 9, 2015 in Cincinnati. TED video, 8:07, https://www.youtube.com/watch?v=EhRXQs0K6ls.

5   Green, Peter, *Alexander of Macedon, 356–323 B.C.: A Historical Biography*, 2013, 85.

A free ebook edition is available with the purchase of this book.

To claim your free ebook edition:

1. Visit MorganJamesBOGO.com
2. Sign your name CLEARLY in the space
3. Complete the form and submit a photo of the entire copyright page
4. You or your friend can download the ebook to your preferred device

Morgan James BOGO™

A **FREE** ebook edition is available for you or a friend with the purchase of this print book.

CLEARLY SIGN YOUR NAME ABOVE

Instructions to claim your free ebook edition:
1. Visit MorganJamesBOGO.com
2. Sign your name CLEARLY in the space above
3. Complete the form and submit a photo of this entire page
4. You or your friend can download the ebook to your preferred device

Print & Digital Together Forever.

Snap a photo

Free ebook

Read anywhere

CPSIA information can be obtained
at www.ICGtesting.com
Printed in the USA
JSHW081720170323
39110JS00002B/2